TYSON HOUSE

THE POWER HOUSE

MORTUARY

STAFF HOUSES

J · A · CHESTON · F R I B A · Associated
C · E · ELCOCK · F R I B A · Architects
ADAM HOUSE · 60 STRAND · W · C · 2.

·1930·

BETHLEM HOSPITAL
1247-1997

A Pictorial Record

Central section of Bethlem Hospital at Moorfields

BETHLEM HOSPITAL 1247-1997

A Pictorial Record

Patricia Allderidge

Phillimore

1997

Published by
PHILLIMORE & CO. LTD.
Shopwyke Manor Barn, Chichester, West Sussex

ISBN 1 86077 054 1

Printed and bound in Great Britain by
BUTLER AND TANNER LTD.
London and Frome

Contents

List of Illustrations

Acknowledgements

I am grateful for permission to reproduce the following illustrations:Crown copyright material in the Public Record Office, reproduced by permission of the Controller of Her Majesty's Stationery Office, 3, 13, 14; The Master and Fellows of Corpus Christi College, Cambridge, 4, 6; The Conway Library, Courtauld Institute of Art, photograph of 6; The Dean and Chapter of St Paul's Cathedral, 5; Arcadian International plc, 11; The British Library, 12, 15, 16; The Museum of London, 18, 38; The Archives and Museum of St Bartholomew's Hospital, 20; The Royal College of Physicians, 43, 50, 57, 75; The National Library of Australia, 91; The Piobaireachd Society, 109; and also to all the staff of the various libraries, archives and museums who have responded so helpfully to my requests for photographs.

I am grateful also to the following: Godfrey New, for photography of most of the archival material and other items; Gina Glover (Photofusion) and the patients involved in the Bethlem photographic project, for no. 195; Diana Leadbetter, for the painting of Bethlem wildlife, no. 182; Byas Mosley & Co., for their generous contribution towards colour printing; Penny Tucker for help in locating some of the medieval material; to all the readers and other visitors to the archives and museum who over the years have introduced me to new aspects of Bethlem's history, and shared their own research with me; and above all to Nicola Willmot, production manager of Phillimore, for her superb skill in keeping this book running on time despite all my attempts to derail it.

I am glad of this opportunity to record my great admiration for and indebtedness to the pioneering historical research which was carried out in the early years of this century by the Rev. Geoffrey O'Donoghue (notwithstanding my occasional critical comments on his literary style). It is particularly appropriate since his *Story of Bethlehem Hospital*, which has stood alone since 1914, will shortly be superceded by the more up-to-date scholarship of *The History of Bethlem* by Jonathan Andrews *et al.*, to be published by Routledge later this year.

Chronology

1247 23 October. The Priory of St Mary of Bethlehem, Bishopsgate, is founded by Simon FitzMary.

1329 First known reference to the priory as a 'hospice' or 'hospital'.

1346 The master of Bethlem appeals to the City of London for protection and patronage. Bethlem's links with the City are first established at this time.

1403 At an enquiry into malpractices at the hospital, it is recorded that there are six insane men in residence there. First reference to Bethlem's use as a hospital for the insane.

1547 13 January. Letters patent of Henry VIII, confirming an agreement of the previous December, grant the 'custody order and government' of the hospital to the City of London.

1553 Foundation of Bridewell Hospital by Edward VI.

1557 Some time after this date, Bridewell and Bethlem are placed under a joint administration which lasts until 1948.

1598 The first complete list of patients is recorded in the governors' minutes.

1634 A visiting physician is appointed. The office of physician to Bethlem is continuous from this time on.

1676 Bethlem moves to a new building at Moorfields, the first custom-built hospital for the insane in this country.

1683 Admission registers begin.

1723/33 Two wings are added to the building, for incurable patients.

1733 Edward Barkham bequeaths an estate in Lincolnshire to support the incurable department.

1770 Indiscriminate visiting by the public is ended by order of the governors.

1815 The report of a Parliamentary Committee appointed to consider 'the better regulation of madhouses in England' reveals abuses and ill treatment at Bethlem and elsewhere.

1815 August. The hospital moves to a new building at St George's Fields, Southwark.

1816 The first State Criminal Lunatic Asylum is opened at Bethlem, under the control of the Home Office.

1838 Building extensions which almost double the accommodation are begun.

1846 The new dome is completed.

1852 The first resident physician superintendent is appointed, and a major programme of reform is begun.

1853 The Lunacy Commissioners are empowered to make regular inspections of the hospital.

1857 Pauper patients are no longer admitted from this time.

1863/64 Criminal patients are transferred to Broadmoor, and the 'criminal wings' demolished.

1870 A convalescent establishment is opened at Witley in Surrey.

1882 Permission is granted by the Charity Commissioners for the first paying patients to be admitted.

1907 Dr. Henry Maudsley offers £30,000 to the London County Council for the establishment of a hospital for early and acute cases of mental illness.

1915 The Maudsley Hospital buildings are completed in Denmark Hill, and handed over for use as a military hospital.

1919 Bethlem opens an outpatients department, the 'Hospital for Nervous Diseases', at 52 Lambeth Road.

1923 The Maudsley Hospital is opened as an LCC mental hospital.

1924 Both Bethlem and the Maudsley are admitted as medical schools of the University of London.

1925 The Monks Orchard Estate is bought by the governors of Bethlem.

1930 The new hospital at Monks Orchard is opened by Queen Mary.

1941 Queen Mary becomes President of Bridewell and Bethlem.

1948 Introduction of the National Health Service. The Bethlem Royal Hospital and the Maudsley Hospital are merged to form a postgraduate psychiatric teaching hospital. The Maudsley's medical school (now the medical school of the joint hospital) becomes the Institute of Psychiatry. Queen Mary becomes patron of the new joint hospital.

1967 The Institute of Psychiatry moves into a new building in De Crespigny Park, adjacent to the Maudsley.

1969 Princess Alexandra becomes patron of the joint hospital.

1982 The Bethlem Royal Hospital and The Maudsley Hospital Special Health Authority replaces the Board of Governors.

1994 The Bethlem and Maudsley NHS Trust is established.

1995 The Trust takes over responsibility for Croydon Mental Health Services, giving Bethlem a local commitment for the first time.

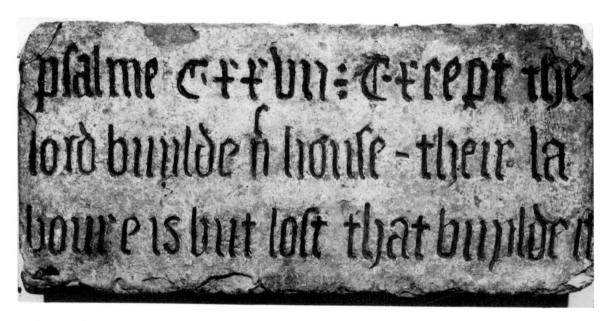

1 *Inscribed stone*

It is not known exactly how this ancient stone came into Bethlem's possession. It was at one time displayed in the entrance hall of the hospital's third building (now the Imperial War Museum), where it was described as having come from the 17th-century building at Moorfields; but it appears to be still earlier in date. Whatever its history may be, the quotation from Psalm 127 aptly symbolises Bethlem's origin as a religious foundation: 'Except the Lord build the house, their labour is but lost that build it'.

I

Bishopsgate

1247-1676

The Foundation

The foundation deed of Bethlem Hospital (now lost, but the original Latin text is preserved in transcripts) is a charter of Simon FitzMary, sealed before witnesses on 23 October 1247:

To all sons of Holy Mother Church to whom this document shall come, Simon son of Mary, citizen of London, sends greetings in the Lord. Amongst other things, indeed above all other things, miraculously performed on earth by high and heavenly counsel, mortal man in his weakness ought to venerate with greater devotion those events which, after the fall of his first ancestor, were the origin of his redemption. Furthermore it seems fitting that he should venerate with particular reverence, and endow with greater benefactions, the place wherein the word made flesh proceeded from the Virgin's womb, who was the author and originator of human redemption. I the said Simon son of Mary, moreover, have a special and single-minded devotion to the Church of the glorious Virgin Mary at Bethlehem. For here the Virgin brought forth her first-born son Jesus Christ, our incarnate Saviour, and fed him with her own milk as he lay in the manger. And here the king and author of our salvation was pleased to be worshipped by the kings, preceeded by a new star as their queen, while a multitude of the heavenly host sang a new hymn for the boy born for us there, 'Glory to God in the Highest'. Therefore out of reverence for Christ and his most blessed mother, and for the honour and prestige of my lord Henry, illustrious king of England (whose wife and children may the aforesaid mother of God and her only begotten son keep under their care and protection), and for the manifold profit of the city of London in which I was born, as also for the salvation of my soul and the souls of my predecessors, successors, kinsmen and friends ... I have given and granted and by this charter of mine confirmed to God and to the Church of Saint Mary of Bethlehem all my land which I held in the parish of Saint Botolph without Bishopsgate in London. That is to say I give them everything I had or may have had there by way of houses, gardens, orchards, fishponds, marshy land and all other appurtenances as enclosed within their boundaries, which extend in length from the King's highway on the east to the ditch on the western part called Deepditch, and in breadth towards the land which was Ralph Dunnyng's towards the north and the land of the Church of St Botolph towards the south; to have and to hold to the aforesaid Church of Bethlehem in free, pure and perpetual alms. And it is my especial wish that a priory should be founded there and that a prior, canons, brothers and also sisters should be constituted, when Jesus Christ has bestowed his grace upon it. And they shall solemnly profess in the said place the rule and order of the said Church of Bethlehem, and they shall wear the sign of the star there both publicly upon their cloaks and mantles and when they celebrate divine service ... and it shall be their particular duty there to receive the bishop of Bethlehem, the canons, brothers and envoys of the Church of Bethlehem for ever, whenever they shall come there ... And since the lord Goffredo de Prefetti, bishop-elect of Bethlehem as confirmed by the Lord Pope, was then in England, I have admitted him into corporeal possession of all the aforesaid properties in his own name and in the name of his successors and of the chapter of the Church of Bethlehem, and I have given him possession of them and he

2 *The Church of St Mary of Bethlehem in Palestine*
Bethlem was founded as a daughter house of the Church of St Mary of Bethlehem (the Cathedral Church of the Nativity) to provide a link with the Holy Land and, more specifically, to create a base in England for the Bethlehemite Order. The Church of the Nativity, built by the Byzantine emperor Justinian, was already over 700 years old in 1247, and the building remains substantially unchanged today. This view was painted by David Roberts in 1839: the church which he visited would be recognisable to Simon FitzMary's contemporaries as well as our own.

has received and taken possession ... and on behalf of myself and my heirs I have most expressly affirmed this gift and the confirmation of this charter of mine and the affixing of my seal. In the Year of Our Lord one thousand two hundred and forty seven, on the Wednesday after the feast of St Luke...

3 *Text of the hospital's foundation deed, from the record of a 'Visitation' in 1403*
Simon FitzMary's original charter of 1247 has not survived, but was transcribed as part of an investigation into the hospital's affairs in 1403. It begins in the third line down, at the extra large word 'Universis'. (Public Record Office: C 270/22.)

4 *'I the said Simon son of Mary have a special and single-minded devotion to the Church of the glorious Virgin Mary at Bethlehem. For here the Virgin brought forth her first-born son Jesus Christ, our incarnate Saviour, and fed him with her own milk as he lay in the manger.'*
The words of FitzMary's deed are reflected in this little nativity scene depicted by his exact contemporary, the chronicler Matthew Paris. Showing the Christ child worshipped by the ox and ass, while his mother reclines watchfully beside him on her four-poster bed, it represents a traditionally domestic view of the stable at Bethlehem. (Matthew Paris, *Chronica Majora*, Parker Library, Corpus Christi College, Cambridge: MS 26.)

4

The document records a grant by FitzMary of his property in Bishopsgate to the Cathedral Church of St Mary of Bethlehem in Palestine (the Church of the Nativity), to found a priory. Apart from his 'special devotion' to the Virgin Mary, he was probably influenced by an actual meeting with Goffredo de Prefetti, the bishop-elect of Bethlehem, who was in England throughout 1247 on a fund-raising mission for his impoverished church. The priory was to provide a base in England for the Order of St Mary of Bethlehem from which to raise further funds for the mother church, and hospitality for visiting members of the Order.

6 (above) *13 October 1247: King Henry III, carrying a holy relic from St Paul's to Westminster Abbey, is met by the bishops, abbots and monks at Westminster*
Pictured again by Matthew Paris, in an eye witness version, this event is closely related to Bethlem's foundation 10 days later. On 13 October a magnificent ceremony was held to receive a relic of the blood of Christ in 'a most beautiful crystal container', sent to England by the patriarch of Jerusalem. The bishop-elect of Bethlehem was present, and Simon FitzMary is likely to have been there. The bishop's fund-raising mission which stirred FitzMary into founding the priory, and the gift of the Holy Blood, were all part of a campaign to restore the fortunes of the church in the east. (Matthew Paris, *Chronica Majora*, Parker Library: MS 16.)

5 (left) *Seal and charter of Simon FitzMary*
FitzMary's seal is here attached to a document which is unconnected with Bethlem, but it would have appeared also on the Bethlem foundation deed. On the side seen here it shows the Virgin and Child, emphasising FitzMary's 'special devotion' to the Virgin Mary which prompted him to found a priory in her honour. His surname means 'son of Mary'. (Guildhall Library, MS 25121/214.)

7 *Plaque on the wall of the* Great Eastern Hotel, *Liverpool Street*
This is all that remains above ground to remind us of where the Priory of St Mary of Bethlehem once stood, and where it remained as 'Bedlam' or Bethlem Hospital until 1676.

8 *Liverpool Street in the early years of this century*
After the hospital had moved and the site known as 'Old Bethlem' had been developed, the principal street was called Bethlem Street. It was renamed in 1825 in honour of the Prime Minister, Lord Liverpool, somewhat to the annoyance of the hospital's governors who had not been consulted. (Bethlem retained the ownership of its original site at Bishopsgate until the 1860s.)

10 *Liverpool Street Station at the turn of the century*

Simon FitzMary was an alderman and twice sheriff of the City of London, a man of substance who owned other properties in the City besides the one in Bishopsgate. In a somewhat turbulent career he undoubtedly made enemies, and may on occasion have taken the royalist side in the disputes which frequently erupted between the king and the City governors. In the Bethlem foundation deed he manages to slip in a few conciliatory words to both sides, but it is impossible now to guess what political motives may have mingled with the genuine piety which seems to show through the formal language of his charter. It can be fairly certain, however, that he had no thought of founding a hospital for the mentally disordered.

9 (left inset) *The Great Eastern Railway: medallion on the railings at Liverpool Street Station*
Much of the Old Bethlem site at Bishopsgate was eventually sold to the Great Eastern Railway Company for the building of Liverpool Street Station. The Company ran into difficulties and almost failed to complete the purchase, which dragged on from 1865 to 1870.

11 (above) *Dining room of the* Great Eastern Hotel
The splendid interiors of the *Great Eastern* are a far cry from the humble monastic building whose remains lie beneath its foundations.

Priory into Hospital

FitzMary's land was on the west side of Bishopsgate street, immediately north of St Botolph's church, a site now covered by Liverpool Street Station. Here Bethlem was built and remained for its first four hundred years. Its operation as a priory seems to have been shortlived, but it did become established as a religious house of some kind, with a master and brothers and sisters, if not the prior and canons envisaged at the foundation. From merely collecting and distributing alms, it began also to provide shelter for the sick and infirm, as well as accommodation for travellers. From the 1330s onwards it is generally referred to in documents as a 'hospital', though at the start this might mean no more than a hospice or hostel. The names 'Bethlem', and the more notorious 'Bedlam' by which it was known for centuries, are just two of many medieval variants of the original 'Bethlehem'. Others include Bedlehem, Betleem, Bethelem and Beddeleem.

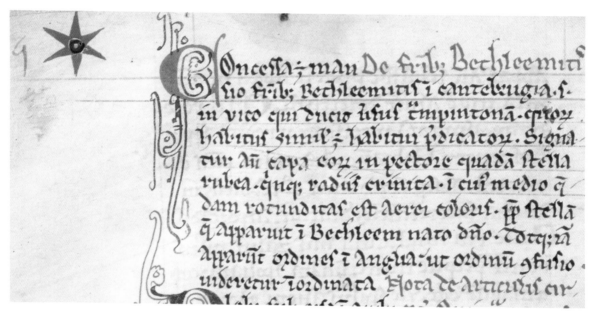

12 *The star of Bethlehem*
Simon FitzMary's foundation deed required the future prior and brethren to wear 'the sign of the star' on their cloaks and mantles. The star which led the wise men from the east was a special symbol of the church of Bethlehem and its religious order. This drawing by Matthew Paris shows the star as worn in 1257 by a community of Bethlehemite brothers in Cambridge. Puzzlingly, he shows it with six rays but describes it in the text as having five, with a circle in the middle 'the colour of the sky'. (The star features prominently in the arms of Bethlem Hospital: see p.35.) (Matthew Paris, *Chronica Majora*, British Library Department of Manuscripts: ROY 14 C. VII.)

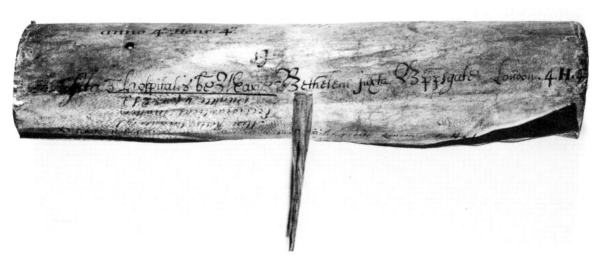

13 *Record of the 'Visitation' of Bethlem, 1403*
This small parchment scroll, now kept in the Public Record Office, has added greatly to our knowledge of Bethlem in the early days of its use as a hospital. It is the record of a royal commission sent by King Henry IV to investigate a long-standing series of scandals and malpractices, and in particular the frauds and embezzlements, extortions, gambling, immorality, and general ill conduct of the porter, Peter Taverner. (Public Record Office: C270/22.)

14 *The first reference to insane patients at Bethlem*
The evidence of witnesses examined during the 1403 enquiry provides much information about Bethlem and its management (or mismanagement) at this time, including the fact that there were insane men among the inmates and lodgers. The passage shown here contains evidence of the accused Peter Taverner himself, to the effect that there were '*sex viri mentecapti et tres alii infirmi*' ('six insane men and three other infirm people') in residence. The words appear in the fourth line from the top. (Public Record Office: C270/22.)

15 *Entry relating to Bethlem, from a mid-15th-century commonplace book*

This commonplace book is thought to have been compiled by William Gregory, who was Lord Mayor of London in 1451. The writer (whoever he was) copied into the book a list of all the churches of the City of London, but in some cases, such as the Bethlem entry, he has added comments of his own: 'A Chyrche of oure lady that ys namyde Bedlem And yn that place ben founde many men that ben fallyn owte of hyr wytte And fulle honestely they ben kepte in that place And sum ben restoryde unto hyr wytte and helthe a gayne And sum ben a bydyng there yn for evyr for they ben falle soo moche owte of hem selfe that hyt ys uncurerabylle unto man …'. (British Library Department of Manuscripts: EG 1995.)

16 *Seal of the wardens [?] of St Mary of Bethlem*

This is a modern impression of a now lost seal, probably early 16th-century in date. At the centre the Virgin, crowned and seated on a high-backed chair, presents the infant Jesus to the three kings. A star hovers overhead. Above a gothic canopy is the star of Bethlehem itself, with six spindly rays and a cross at its centre. At the bottom of the seal, below a straw-filled manger, are the upside down heads of an ox and an ass. The imagery of the nativity is a clear reminder of the hospital's origins. Unfortunately the Latin inscription surrounding it, which includes the unknown word 'wardones', leaves some doubt as to precisely who used this seal. (British Library Department of Manuscripts: Seal LXXVIII.3.)

17 (left) *Early fundraising: certificate of admission to the confraternity of St Mary of Bethlehem, 1519*

This certificate granted admission to the confraternity of the Blessed Mary of Bethlehem, along with certain indulgences and remission of sins, to those who contributed to the hospital's funds. It was issued by the Master, John Cavalari. Donors are reminded that they are giving support to the

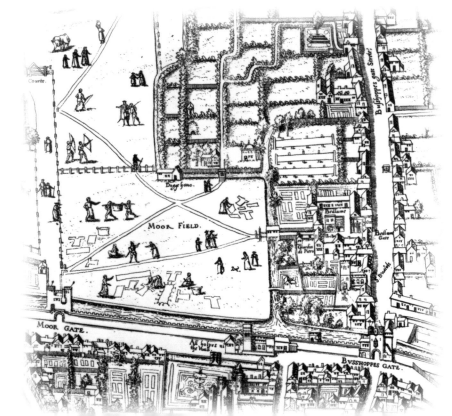

...myde Bedleem And yn that palace ben founde many
that ben fallyn owte of hyr wytte And fulle
eftely they ben kepte in that place And sum
restoryde vnto hyr wytte and helthe agayne
... sum ben a bydyng there yn for euyr for they
falle soo moche owte of hem selfe that hyt ys
vncurabylle vnto man And vnto that place ys
... mytyde moche pardon more thenne they of the
... knowe

Synt Mary Spettylle a poore pryory and
a Parysshe Chyrche in the same
And that pryory kepyth ospytalyte
for poore men And sum first systers
yn the same place to kepe the boddys
that come oont for poore men that
come to that place

The Parysshe Chyrche of Ortardyches.
The subbarbys a oowte Algate
And the Chyrchys that longyn
there to
a parysshe Chyrche i namyd wyyte
the menoros Abbay
a parysshe Chyrche w' in the same
The wyyte Abbay att the toure Hylle
Synt Kateryns
And yn that othyr party ys a place
of Nunnys i callyd Halywelle

The first evidence that the hospital was being used to house insane patients dates from 1403, and it is unlikely that the practice began much earlier. It has been suggested that a house at Charing Cross was previously used for the purpose, and that the inmates were removed to Bethlem because an unspecified 'king of England' did not like them so near to his palace. The transfer, if not the reason, seems possible, and the hospital did own a property at Charing Cross from around this time: but the exact details of how Bethlem began caring for the mentally disordered seem likely to remain a mystery. On any estimation, however, it appears now to be the oldest psychiatric hospital in Europe to be still in use.

18 (below) *Map of the Moorfields area, c.1559 (detail)*
This surviving section of a lost pictorial map of London shows 'Bedlame' in Bishopsgate 300 years after its foundation. It is the earliest representation that we have of the hospital buildings. Bethlem stood beside one of the the main north/south routes through the City of London, leading northwards to the Great North Road and southwards across London Bridge. Situated just outside the City walls, it was well placed to provide accommodation for travellers, and later to develop into a hospital for the poor and sick.

church and the buildings 'as well as … the insane, the mad, the frenzied, and others residing in the same places, who are there lodged and cared for with great diligence and attention …'. There is also reference to such people receiving medical attention and sometimes being cured, but at this point (if not before) the corrupt Latin text defies precise translation. (This illustration is a 19th-century facsimile of an original certificate.)

The King and the City

Around the middle of the 14th century, at the request of the then master, the City of London began to supervise Bethlem's affairs to some extent, though at this stage probably only in financial matters. Later in the century the king seized the hospital as an 'alien priory', and a dispute arose as to who really controlled it which rumbled on for nearly two centuries. In 1547 King Henry VIII finally granted the government of Bethlem to the City. In this move it became both a City institution and a 'royal' hospital, a resolution which might well have satisfied the ambivalent loyalties of the founder, and remained

19 *Anne Boleyn, sister of the Master of Bethlem* George Boleyn, brother of the more famous Anne, was appointed Master of Bethlem Hospital in 1529, one of many offices which fell his way during the king's courtship of his sister. He retained it until his dramatic arrest, trial and execution, along with the queen, in 1536. The right to appoint the master of Bethlem had long been in dispute between the king and the City. The City was shortly to gain control, and Boleyn was among the last of the masters to receive the office as a royal favour (and also the first and last to lose it on the scaffold).

20 *Deed of Covenant for the refoundation of St Bartholomew's Hospital*
In December 1546 King Henry VIII completed a detailed agreement with the citizens of London for the refoundation of St Bartholomew's Hospital, seized during the dissolution of the religious houses. In a brief passage in the same document it was agreed in passing 'that the said Mayor and Commonaltie and Citizens [of London] … shall be masters rulers and governors of the hospital or house called Bethelem …' and that they should have the 'order rule and governance' of Bethlem 'and of the people there'. (The entire Bethlem section occupies three lines near the bottom of the document.) On 13 January 1547, shortly before his death, the king confirmed the whole agreement by charter, but this preliminary covenant forms the real body of the transaction.

under the formal governorship of the City until taken over by the National Health Service in 1948.

Other institutions passing to the City around this time were the former monastic hospitals of St Bartholomew and St Thomas, re-founded by Henry VIII and Edward VI, and Christ's Hospital and Bridewell, new foundations of Edward VI. Together with Bethlem these became the five Royal Hospitals of the City of London (though Bethlem did not actually start using the word 'Royal' as part of its name until late in the 19th century). Bethlem's administration seems to have been kept separate from the other hospitals at first, but by the 1570s it had been placed under a joint management with Bridewell, which also lasted until 1948.

Under this arrangement one president, treasurer and court of governors handled the business of both hospitals. The governors themselves came from the City's own governing bodies, the Court of Aldermen and the Court of Common Council. Later, an increasing number were drawn from outside, but ultimate control always remained firmly in the hands of the City, and the president himself had generally served as Lord Mayor.

21 *Portrait of King Henry VIII, attributed to the circle of Hans Holbein*
By granting the 'governance' of Bethlem to the City of London Henry VIII finally relinquished the crown's claim to patronage of the hospital, a claim which probably dated back to the 1370s. He later came to be regarded either as Bethlem's actual founder, or at least as having first established it as a hospital for the insane. This portrait is known to have hung in the committee room of the second hospital, and was said to have been 'brought from old Bethlem', but nothing more is known about how or when it was acquired.

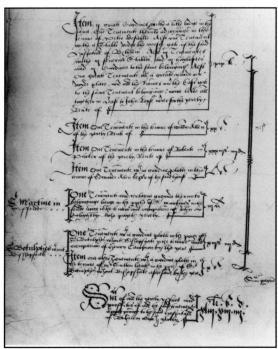

22 (facing page, top) *Bridewell Hospital, founded 1553 (as it was rebuilt after the Great Fire)*
Bridewell Hospital was founded by King Edward VI, and occupied the former royal palace of Bridewell, fronting onto the Thames at Blackfriars. This was largely destroyed in the Great Fire of 1666. Although intended as a workhouse, it actually functioned mainly as a prison for petty offenders until the 19th century. It also trained apprentices in various trades, and this aspect of its work developed into King Edward's School (now at Witley in Surrey) after the closure of the prison. Bridewell was the headquarters of the joint administration of Bridewell and Bethlem, and the governors met there.

23 (facing page, left) *Part of a rental of property owned by Bethlem in 1555*
The total value of the rents is shown as 'xliijli.. xiijs.. iiijd..', or £43 13s. 4d.

24 (facing page, right) *The Order of the Hospitals of King Henry VIII and King Edward VI, 1557*
This little book of ordinances, drawn up by the City of London for the administration of its newly acquired hospitals, is notable for the omission of Bethlem. The other four hospitals had their own governors, officers, and rules; but for nearly a century Bethlem went on being farmed out to a 'keeper' (replacing the former master), only gradually coming under the control of the governors of Bridewell. As with other aspects of Bethlem's early history, the exact details of why and how this took place may never be known.

25 (right) *List of patients in Bethlem, 1598*
The governors, meeting at Bridewell, left Bethlem largely in the hands of the keeper at this time. In December 1598 a committee was appointed 'to view the house at Bethalem [sic] where the lunatic people are kept ...', and investigate the state of neglect into which it had fallen. They found it 'so loathsomly and filthely kept, not fitt for anye man to come into the sayd howse'. As part of their enquiry they made this list of all 20 patients in the hospital, noting who was responsible for their keep. It is the first complete list of patients. Significantly they are here called 'prisoners', probably reflecting the governors' greater familiarity with Bridewell and its terminology.

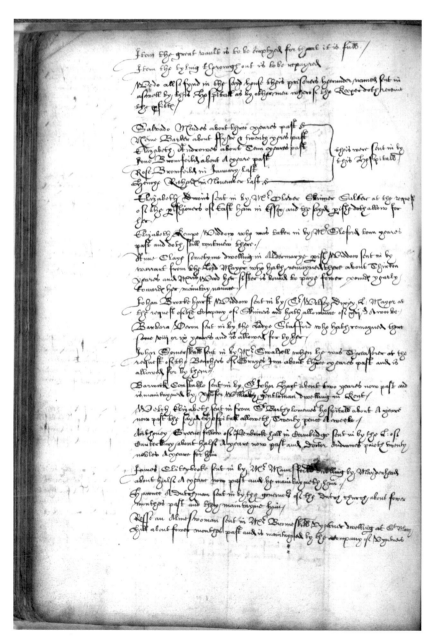

The 17th Century

Over the centuries Bethlem has had cycles of decline and regeneration, and the early days of the partnership with Bridewell seem to have been a particularly bad period. The business of Bridewell took up most of the governors' attention, and Bethlem and its patients suffered seriously from neglect. It was often overcrowded, despite enlargements in the 17th century which nearly trebled the accommodation from the original twenty or so: and the development of the Bethlem precinct as a source of income led to the hospital itself becoming hemmed in by other buildings. Since 1247, Bishopsgate had changed from an open environment with a few large houses to an area which was increasingly crammed with small and sub-divided premises, often commercial or industrial. By the mid-17th century it had become congested, noisy and polluted.

26 *17th-century tavern token*
Token coins are known from several taverns, eg. the *Sun*, the *Half Moon* and the *Pump*, within the Bethlem precinct in Bishopsgate, which saw much commercial development during the 17th century. Worth a farthing each, they were issued by landlords for the use of their own customers. The one shown here is inscribed on one side 'AT THE SUNE IN BEDLAM', and on the other 'EPHRAIM CLITHEROW'.

Strange and VVonderfull
PROPHESIES
BY
The Lady ELEANOR AUDELEY; who
is yet alive, and lodgeth in WHITE-HALL.

Which Shee Prophesied sixteen yeeres agoe, and had them Printed in Holland, and there presented the said Prophesies to the Prince Elector; For which she was imprisoned seven yeers here in *England*, by the late King and his Majesties Councell : First, she was put into the Gate-house then into Bedlam, and afterwards into the Tower of LONDON.

With Notes upon the said Prophesies, how farre they are fulfilled, and what part remains yet unfulfilled, concerning the late King, and Kingly Government, and the Armies and people of ENGLAND. And particularly White-Hall, and other wonderfull Predictions.

Imprimatur Theodore Jennings August 25. 1649.

London Printed for Robert Ibbitson in Smithfield near the
Queens head Tavern, 1649.

27 *Strange and Wonderfull Prophesies by The Lady Eleanor Audeley [Davies], 1649*
On 28 July 1625 Lady Eleanor Davies, daughter of Lord Audeley, was 'Awakened by a voyce from HEAVEN', and heard the following message: 'there is Nineteene yeares and a halfe to the day of Judgement and you as the meek Virgin'. Thereafter she devoted her life to publishing her prophesies, producing over sixty tracts. She was several times imprisoned (a common fate of prophets), and was confined in Bethlem for over a year.

28 *Lady Eleanor in Bethlem: entry from the minutes of the Court of Governors, 28 February 1638*
Lady Eleanor was declared insane by the Privy Council and sent to Bethlem after vandalising the altar of Lichfield Cathedral by pouring hot tar and wheat paste on it, and sitting on the bishop's throne to declare herself Primate and Metropolitan. (Her act is reminiscent, or perhaps prophetic, of Jonathan Martin's still more dramatic gesture at York two centuries later.) At Bethlem she was housed with the Steward, Richard Langley, rather than with the other patients, an arrangement which had its drawbacks. In the entry shown here it is recorded that Langley and his wife are accused of being 'very unquiet uncivell and ungoverned people, and that they doe very oftentimes come home both together very farre gone in drincke and that 11. and 12. of Clocke at night and then very much disturbe the Lady Davies who is prisoner in their house …'.

29 *Daniel, Oliver Cromwell's porter*
Daniel, also a prophet, was another of Bethlem's more notable patients. A giant in stature (his height was said to have been marked with a large 'O' on a terrace at Windsor Castle), he was allowed to have his library in Bethlem with him. This included a large Bible reputedly given to him by Nell Gwyn. Followers gathered on a grass plot outside his window to hear him preach, as an eye-witness recounted: 'I saw some women, very busie with their *Bibles*, turning to the Quotations, as he *Preach'd* to them out of the Window; and they did Sigh and Groan, and shew'd as strong motions of Devotion as cou'd be seen at any *Quaker Meeting*'. (Although this anecdote places Daniel in the Moorfields building, he was originally admitted while the hospital was still at Bishopsgate.)

M. Lauron ad vivam del.   *W.T. Taylor sculp.*

Oliver Cromwell's Porter

Published by I. Caulfield 1793

30 *Minutes of the first meeting of the Court of Governors to be held at Bethlem, 14 September 1666*
The opening entry records that 'Whereas the Hospitall of Bridewell London by a firce [*sic*] and lamentable fire was lately burnt and consumed withall buildings and much wares and goods therein ...', it was decided that until further notice '... on every Friday weekely ... A Courte shalbe holden att this hospitall of Bethlem att Nyne of the Clocke in the forenoone ... '. Deprived of their meeting place in a former royal palace overlooking the Thames, the governors were forced to meet for the next three years in a decrepit former monastery amidst the less salubrious surroundings of Bishopsgate, often rendered noisome by their own tenants. This clearly gave them something to think about.

18

◆

II

Moorfields

1676-1815

Rebuilding

The Great Fire of 1666 did not reach Bishopsgate, but destroyed most of Bridewell. Soon after Bridewell had been restored it was decided that Bethlem too should be rebuilt, about half a mile to the west at Moorfields. A site was chosen just north of a surviving section of the old London Wall, consisting of a strip of land 740 feet from east to west and 80 feet deep. After some negotiation, the president Sir William Turner triumphantly announced to his fellow governors on 9 October 1674 that he had secured a lease from the City of London for 999 years at a nominal rent of 12 pence a year, provided they keep a hospital standing on the land. (This turned out to be an over estimate of requirements by about 858 years.)

31 *Spital Sermon, delivered before the Lord Mayor and Aldermen by the Rev. Simon Ford, Preacher to Bridewell Hospital, 1672*
The Spital (or Spittle) Sermons were preached annually at Easter, to encourage charitable giving and to remind the City fathers of their duties towards all the Royal Hospitals. On this occasion the preacher took the opportunity 'to recommend to you, the *New-Building ...* of your *Hospital of Bethlem ...*'.

> *The blessedness of being bountiful.* 133
> ped, the *blessedness*, you have already (according to my Text) found in your past Beneficences, will encourage you (beyond all the Rhetorick which, if I had it, I could bestow on such an Argument,) to go on, and effectually promote such further designs, as shall be suggested to you for the rendring them more usefull to the ends of these several Foundations.
> And here give me leave, (I beseech you) *first* of all, to recommend to you, the *New-Building*, (among all the famous Structures that your City hath raised for publick uses since the last dreadfull fire) of your *Hospital of Bethlem*: which I doe upon this consideration, that those who have the particular Inspection of that Hospital, (and especially, that learned and diligent *Physician* who can hardly be valued sufficiently for his great skill, fidelity
> K 3 lity

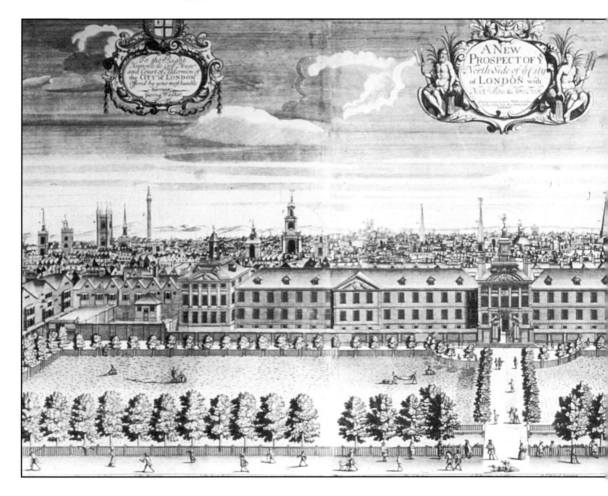

The new building was designed by Robert Hooke, a friend of Christopher Wren with whom he collaborated on many buildings, and one of the surveyors appointed for rebuilding the City after the fire. It was originally intended for 120 patients, but when completed it held slightly more. The enormous length of this building (estimates vary, but it seems to have been at least 550 feet long), and its magnificent appearance facing north across the elegant walks and open vistas of Moorfields, made it one of London's tourist attractions. It featured in numerous topographical works and guidebooks, was frequently engraved, and inspired a number of poems. It also inspired a good deal of comment, often unfavourable, on the notion of building a 'palace' for the accommodation of poor lunatics.

32 *The first steps towards rebuilding: entry from the minutes of the Court of Governors, 23 January 1674*
'Alsoe This Courte takeing into Considerac[i]on that the Hospitall House of Bethlem is very old weake & ruinous and to [*sic*] small & streight for keepeing the greate numb[er] of Lunatikes as are therein att p[re]sent and more are often needfull to be sent thither Itt is ordered that all the Governo[r]s be sum[m]oned as A Com[m]ittee to conside[er] thereof and whether the same House may sufficiently be repaired and inlarged or must be newbuilt & inlarged ...' Eventually the decision was taken that it must be 'newbuilt'.

33 *'New Bedlam' in Moorfields, designed by Robert Hooke, opened in 1676*
The new building, the first custom-built hospital for the insane in this country, was at least 550 feet long, lavishly ornamented, and intended to impress. The governors gave much attention to its appearance, to the gratings in the wall which would enable its 'grace and ornament' to be better seen, to the pineapples which topped the wall, and the 'cubiloes' (cupolas) which topped the building. Hooke leant heavily on French models for the overall design, but Dutch influence is seen in some of the details. The wings were brick with stone dressings, while the pavilions were all in stone and embellished with corinthian pilasters, swags, wreaths, armorial bearings, festoons, balconies, balustrades, lanterns, and a clock with 'three fair dials' surmounted by a gilded ball and a dragon weather vane. The arms of Henry VIII, of the City of London, of the president Sir William Turner, and of the hospital itself were prominently displayed. The royal arms in the central pediment caused the governors much anxiety, in case they were not made 'as well & spacious as the place there will possibly admit', and nearly had to be taken down and made bigger. (A wise concern, perhaps, since King Charles himself was soon to pay a visit.)

34 *Caius Gabriel Cibber, 1630-1700*

Cibber's statues for the entrance gates of the second hospital are almost all that has survived from this building. Danish born, Cibber settled in England and became one of the leading sculptors of his day. For the City of London, he also carved the bas relief at the base of the Monument, and towards the end of his life made several carvings for Wren at St Paul's, including the great phoenix over the south door. His son, the actor and playwright Colley Cibber, singled out the Bethlem figures as being 'no ill monuments of [my father's] fame as an artist', and they have long been acclaimed as his finest and most original work.

35 *(below left and right) Figures known as 'Raving and Melancholy Madness', by C.G. Cibber*
These massive figures in Portland stone rested over the gateposts of the main entrance, stark symbols of the grim reality within. Surprisingly, especially given the governors' preoccupation with the hospital's appearance, the records contain no mention of them until long after they had been erected.

Already by 1717 they were being celebrated in verse (*Bethlem Hospital. A Poem in Blank Verse*, printed for E. Smith in Cornhill):

> ... Here far beyond or what the Roman Art
> Or Graecian cou'd perform, sad Frantick Minds
> In stone by Cibbers Matchless forming Hand
> Express'd, You see, and Wondering praise his skills ...

Alexander Pope later used them in *The Dunciad* to scoff at Colley Cibber: 'Where o'er the gates, by his fam'd father's hand / Great Cibber's brazen, brainless brothers stand': but even here he acknowledges the father's 'fame'.

Despite the supposedly healthy air of Moorfields (*see* p.24) and protection by thick layers of paint, the statues have been quite badly eroded, and were at one time blackened by air pollution. In the 1770s they were threatened with restoration, which would almost certainly have amounted to re-cutting, but were found to be already too far 'damaged and impaired' by exposure to the weather. They were brought indoors when Bethlem moved to its third site, but by 1858 had fallen out of favour and were banished to the South Kensington (now Victoria and Albert) Museum, though remaining the property of the hospital and subject to recall. Later they progressed to the new Guildhall Museum, and did not return to Bethlem until more than a century after leaving it. Now in Bethlem's own museum, they have been cleaned of their paint and other accretions, and show the remains of Cibber's original surface. (The statues are shown here in the Guildhall Museum in the 1920s.)

Inside it consisted principally of two huge galleries one above the other, broken only by openwork iron grilles in the central area which left an unobstructed view the full length of the building. Men were housed in the east end, women in the west. The site had been chosen 'for health and air', and the design of the building was calculated to enhance these features. In front was the great space of Moorfields itself. (The part immediately in front of the hospital is now Finsbury Circus.) Individual cells for the patients opened off the galleries on one side only, leaving the galleries well lit by windows along the north wall; and the undivided galleries, 16 feet wide, allowed the healthy Moorfields air to circulate freely. At either end of the building was a high-walled exercise yard, in which such of the patients 'as are capable' were allowed to walk in the even fresher air outdoors.

36 *Replicas of 17th-century almsboxes*
The original painted wooden almsboxes (these are fibreglass replicas) were given to Bethlem by a merchant, Mr. Foote, in 1676. The figures hold bottles with slots into which the money was placed, dropping down into the pedestals. They stood in niches just inside the entrance, beneath the inscription 'Pray remember the poor lunaticks, and put your charity into the box with your own hand'. The originals remained in Bethlem until 1921 when they mysteriously escaped into the collection of Sir Henry Wellcome, and are now part of the Wellcome Collection at the Science Museum.

37 (above) *Bethlehem's Beauty ... A Panegyrical Poem, 1676*
This hundred-line poem was the first of many panegyrical outpourings on the wonders of new Bethlem. The anonymous author (Roger L'Strange whose name appears at the top was only the licensee) was particularly quick off the mark, and the poem was licensed within weeks of the hospital's opening. He claimed that 'So Brave, so Neat, so Sweet it does appear, / Makes one Half-Madd to be a Lodger there.' The sight of new Bethlem did not always produce such satisfactory results. Thomas Brown, writing at the turn of the century, felt that 'the outside is perfect mockery to the inside, and admits of two amusing queries, Whether the persons that ordered the building of it, or those that inhabit it, were the maddest?'

38 (top right) *Silver flagon presented to the treasurer of Bridewell and Bethlem, 1677*
This is one of a pair of flagons presented to Benjamin Ducane by his fellow governors, in consideration of his 'greate & extraordinary paynes Care and faithfullnesse ... in the affaires of the Hospitall of Bridewell & Bethlem and that Twoe yeares past hee hath imployed most of his tyme in carrying on the Newbuilding of the said Hospitall of Bethlem w[i]th all imaginable diligence ...', and as 'a Testimony of the Love & Respect of the Governors of the said Hospitalls unto him and as a thankfull Acknowledgem[en]t of his Faithfullnesse Love Care & paynes for the said Hospitall'.

39 (bottom right) *Restraint: bill for smith's work, 1697*
Amongst such everyday items as a key for the hatch, mending a poker for the steward's room, and two springs for the 'pallisadoes gates', this bill for work done by the smith in 1697 contains chillingly casual references to 'mending the lock for a woman's foot', and 'filing off the lock of a woman's foot'. Physical restraint by chains, manacles and leg irons was a commonplace until the early 19th century, when it began to be phased out.

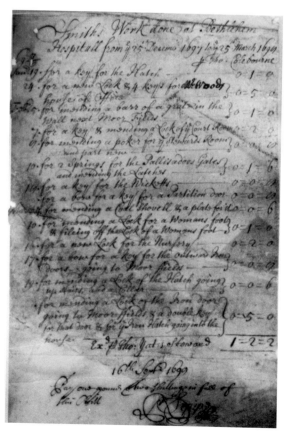

40 *Dr. Edward Tyson*
Dr. Tyson was physician to Bethlem from 1684 until his death in 1708. Though the post was only that of 'visiting' physician (and remained so until the 1850s), Tyson seems to have shown exceptional devotion to his duties at the hospital. After 10 years in office, he was credited by the governors with curing a greater number of patients than had ever been cured before. His regime saw the introduction of warm and cold baths for therapeutic use, the first nurse appointed to care for the patients' bodily ailments, and a fund set up to provide clothes and other necessities for the poor and friendless on their discharge. He also inaugurated a fund for medicines to be dispensed on an outpatient basis to discharged patients, to prevent their relapse. His name was originally attached to the after-care fund, but is now more permanently commemorated in the naming of Tyson House.

41 *The charge to every governor on his admission*
The 'charge' was administered by the chaplain to each new governor on his first attendance at a meeting of the Court of Governors, and reminded him that he had been elected to 'a station of great honour and trust, which will afford you many opportunities of promoting the glory of God and the welfare of your fellow creatures'. It was written around 1707 by Francis Atterbury, later Bishop of Rochester, when he was preacher to Bridewell Hospital. (This illuminated version is obviously a later production.)

42 *London penny token*
A token coin issued by the City of London, showing Bethlem Hospital as one of London's famous buildings.

Patients considered fit to do so were also allowed to walk in the galleries, after an initial period when this was prohibited, though many were kept locked in their cells even by day: but the galleries were chiefly notable for being thronged with visitors and sightseers, not all of whom were there for benign purposes. Some had genuinely come to see friends or relatives: others at least kept up the pretence that such visits were morally instructive, arousing charity and compassion in the spectator: but many undoubtedly went there for mere entertainment, teasing and provoking those unfortunate inmates who did not already appear to be sufficiently entertaining in their own right. Indiscriminate visiting by the public was not stopped until 1770.

43 *Dr. James Monro, physician to Bethlem Hospital 1728-1752, founder of the Monro dynasty at Bethlem: portrait by John Michael Williams, 1747*
James Monro was the first of four members of his family to hold the post of physician to Bethlem in a succession which lasted until 1853. He became known as the leading 'mad-doctor' of his period, a reputation which appears to have rested largely on his position at Bethlem rather than any identifiable contribution to this branch of medicine. In the words of his son, he believed 'that the management requisite for [insanity] was never to be learned but by observation ... he never thought of reading lectures, on a subject that can be understood no otherwise than by personal observation'.

Within the image:
54
55
50

Madness, Thou Chaos of ye Brain, | With Rule disjointed, shapeless Measure, | Shapes of Pleasure, that but Seen | The headstrong course of youth thus run, See Him by Thee to Ruin
that are, That Pleasure givest and Pain | Filld with Horror, filld with Pleasure, | Would split the shaking Sides of Spleen | What Comfort from this darling Son: And curse thy self, & curse
Tyranny of Fancy's Reign | Shapes of Horror, that wou'd even | O Vanity of Age: here See | Tis rattling Chains with Horror hear,
Mechanic Fancy, that can build | cast Doubt of Mercy upon Heaven. | The Stamp of Heaven effac'd by Thee | Behold Death grappling with Despair.
ist Labyrinths, & Mazes wild.

Invented by Wm Hogarth & Publish'd according to Act of Parliament June ye 25 1735

44 *The interior of Bethlem: the final scene from* A Rake's Progress *by William Hogarth, 1735*
This often reproduced scene is the only authentic (more or less) picture of the interior of Bethlem known to exist before the middle of the 19th century. It has been said to represent one of the new wings for 'incurables', but the continuation of the gallery in a single line beyond the grille suggests that this is actually the main hospital, as do other features. In the foreground are the participants in Hogarth's tale, but two figures in the group are probably intended for members of the hospital's staff. The man removing the Rake's leg irons is presumably a keeper (or 'basketman' as male keepers were then called), while the man standing behind may be the apothecary or the physician. A number of patients are at liberty in the gallery, while others are confined to their straw-filled beds (proper bedding was in fact also in use by this time). In the background are two female visitors. One pretends to hide her eyes in mock modesty from the sight of the urinating 'King', while her maid draws attention to him.

45 (above left) *Edward Barkham of Wainfleet St Mary and Lincoln, a major benefactor*
Over the centuries Bethlem acquired property in various parts of the country, mostly through donations and bequests, which helped to support its charitable work. The largest single gift was an agricultural estate of nearly 3,000 acres in Lincolnshire, mainly in the parish of Wainfleet St Mary, which was left to the hospital by Edward Barkham specifically for 'the further and better Support Reliefe and Maintenance of poor Incurable Lunaticks'. Barkham died in 1733, and the Lincolnshire estate was the mainstay of the newly established 'incurable department' (*see* p.32) from that time until its closure early in the present century. The estate was sold in 1919.

46 (above right) *Mary, wife of Edward Barkham*

47 (right) *Medieval title deed relating to land in Wainfleet St Mary, c.1200*
Although Bethlem did not acquire its Lincolnshire estate until the 1730s and sold it in 1919, a large number of medieval deeds were acquired with the property, and remain in the archives today. This small parchment deed recording a grant of land from Rengot of Wainfleet to Thomas son of Herward is the oldest document in the hospital's possession, predating Bethlem itself.

Sr

Have sent by Smith a Hamper of my best apples, should have sent some Rumb but coud gett none when the West India Fleet came in. Design to pay a hundred pounds or half a years rent as soon as my Hopps w[ch] are at London are sold, which I expect to hear every day and have done some time, shall send some more as soon as begin to Thrash for Sale having thrashed none but for Seed

from your humble Servant

Jn[o] Gurney

Cottington
Novem[r]: 1st 1747

48 (above) *A water seller on the Bethlem estate at Wainfleet, 1911*

49 (left) *Letter from the tenant of Cottington Court Farm, 1747*
Cottington Court Farm, near Deal in Kent, was acquired as one of Bethlem's endowment estates in 1683, and sold in 1958. In the 18th century it was farmed by the Gurney family. This letter from John Gurney to Joseph Taylor, clerk to the governors, illustrates the hand-to-mouth existence of the tenant farmer. Enclosing a hamper of his best apples and apologising for not being able to send any rum, he plans to send half a year's rent as soon as his hops are sold, and some more as soon as he begins to thrash his corn. Gurney's difficulties with his rent, and his propitiatory offerings of apples, hams, brandy and rum, can be traced through a long series of similar communications.

50 (right) *Dr. John Monro, physician to Bethlem Hospital 1752-91: portrait by Nathaniel Dance 1769*

John Monro succeeded his father as physician to Bethlem on the latter's death. He opened a private asylum at Brooke House in Hackney, which remained in use until it was bombed in 1940, and the contrasting care received by the Monros' private patients and their patients in Bethlem came to public attention in the early 19th century. Like his father, he believed that the treatment of insanity could only be learned by observation (and by being born a Monro); but he was provoked by the 'undeserved censures', which Dr. Battie of St Luke's Hospital had passed on his family's methods, into publishing a small booklet on the subject called *Remarks on Dr Battie's Treatise on Madness*. It opens with the memorable declaration that 'madness is a distemper of such a nature, that very little of real use can be said concerning it'.

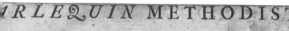

51 (left) *Harlequin Methodist, 1763*
This satire on the early methodist preachers, who frequented Moorfields, is set against the instantly recognisable backdrop of Bethlem Hospital.

The patients considered most suitable for admission were (as noted in the 1720 edition of Stow's *Survey of London*) 'those ... that are raving and furious, and capable of Cure; or if not, yet are likely to do mischief to themselves or others; and are Poor, and cannot be otherwise provided for'. In earlier times, patients who did not recover had sometimes stayed for many years, though Bethlem has always been a true hospital in the modern sense that patients were admitted in order to be cured if possible. In the new hospital, it became the rule that those showing no sign of recovery after 12 months would be discharged uncured. This led to obvious difficulties, and in the 1720s and '30s two wings were added at either end of the building to house a limited number of 'incurable' patients. Provision was made for 50 each of men and women, but only those who had already been discharged uncured from the main hospital and for whom no other care could be provided by their family or friends.

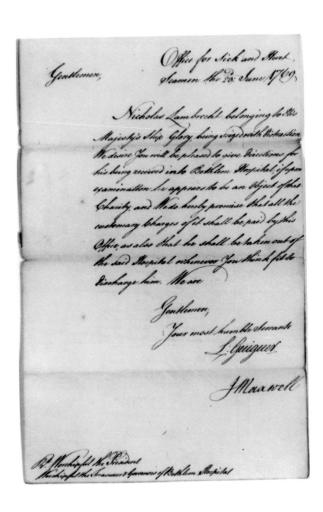

52 (left) *Letter from the Office for Sick and Hurt Seamen requesting the admission of a patient, 1769*
Military and naval patients were sent to Bethlem by, respectively, the Transport Office and the 'Sick and Hurt' or 'Sick and Wounded' Office. Here a request is being made for the admission of Nicholas Lambrecht of His Majesty's ship *Glory*, who has been 'seized with distraction'. (The admission registers show that Lambrecht was discharged 'well' the following year.)

53 (centre) *18th-century almsbox*
This almsbox, with its slightly exotic pagoda top and generous curves, seems to invite a matching generosity from donors. The money dropped down a chute to a compartment in the base, which was protected by a fearsome array of metal teeth to prevent the less than generous from fishing it back out again. The brass plates are inscribed with the age old caveat to 'Pray Remember the Poor *Lunaticks* and Put Your Charity into this Box With Your Own Hand', a reminder of the likely misappropriation which would occur if you entrusted it to any other hand.

54 (right) *The end of casual visiting: entry from the minutes of the Court of Governors, 21 November 1770*
At this meeting the governors endorsed a memorial from the Grand Committee of Bethlem, to the effect that the present method of admitting visitors led to 'great Irregularities [being] daily Committed the Patients disturbed and often Robbed of their Provisions and Cloaths by the Admission of improper Persons into the Hospital ...'. It was recommended that in future 'no Person or Persons whatsoever, Except a Governor, or in Company with a Governor and the Officers and Servants of the Hospital be Permitted to enter the same, unless he she or they produce to the Porter of said Hospital a Ticket Signed by one of the Governors ...'.

55 *Margaret Nicholson's attempted assassination of King George III, 1786*

Margaret Nicholson was confined in Bethlem from 1786 until her death in 1828, having made a rather half-hearted attempt on the king's life. She was found to be insane after an investigation by the Privy Council assisted by the two Drs Monro of the day, in the course of which she asserted that she had a right to a property due to her from the Crown of England, and if she had it not 'a Woeful War would ensue'; and the Drs Monro asserted that it was perfectly possible to be insane, and still take a hand at whist. This is the largest and most detailed of several prints which interpret the event with varying degrees of drama. In fact, the rather blunt table knife made little impression on the royal waistcoat, and the king gave instructions to 'take care of the woman—do not hurt her, for she is mad'.

56 *Margaret Nicholson: entry in the Bethlem Sub-Committee Minutes, 11 August 1787*

When she had not recovered after a year in Bethlem, the message recorded here was delivered from the king, who 'had been graciously Pleased to Express himself highly Sensible of the great Care and Attention that had been observed by the Governors ... in their Treatment of Margaret Nicholson ...' and wished that she might still be accommodated in the hospital. Not surprisingly, she was promptly admitted to the incurable department.

57 *Dr. Thomas Monro, physician to Bethlem Hospital 1792-1816: portrait by his son Henry Monro (d. aged 24)*

Thomas Monro assisted his father at Bethlem, and succeeded to the post in 1792. He was probably the most distinguished member of the family, though not in the field of medicine. A friend of many leading artists and a talented amateur in his own right, he gave the name of 'Dr Monro's Academy' to the group of young water-colourists who came to his house to copy draw-ings from his huge collection. Turner and Girtin were among his early protégés; others included De Wint, Varley, and Cotman. Thomas Monro did not come well out of the enquiry of the 1815 parliamentary committee (*see* p.42), which exposed many abuses at Bethlem. Under pressure from the committee the governors did not re-elect him to his post in 1816 (though they did replace him with his son Edward Thomas).

58 *The arms of Bethlem Hospital (as they appeared from 1676 to about 1930)*

This painting on parchment hung in the committee room at Moorfields. The small shields round the outside contain the arms of the presidents from 1640 to 1782, with the arms of the City of London at the bottom. Bethlem's arms include the star of Bethlehem in the centre of the blue 'chief', now with 16 rays and a white disc (probably the Host) with a red cross at its centre. The basket of bread on the right may refer to the name 'Bethlehem', meaning in Hebrew 'house of bread'. The scull on the left was a mistake. In 1676 there was confusion as to what the arms should be, and the College of Arms supplied this version: however, a manuscript in the College's collection dating from the early 16th century shows clearly that the symbol was actually a chalice and Host. It was with some relief that the error was discovered and corrected nearly three centuries later. The significance of the lower part of the shield is not known, but the red 'label' is the symbol of a first-born son.

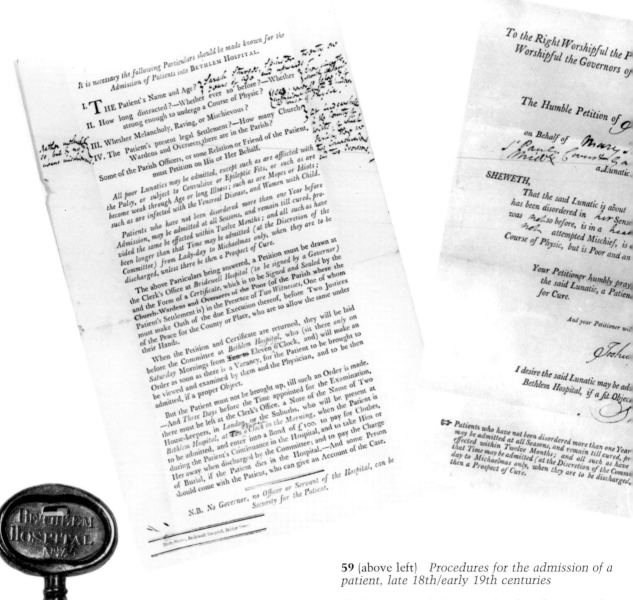

59 (above left) *Procedures for the admission of a patient, late 18th/early 19th centuries*

60 (above centre) *Petition for the admission of a patient, 1800*
The petition was the first stage in the admission procedure. At this date no medical certificate was required. The petition was considered at the weekly Bethlem Sub-Committee, which was always attended by the physician. Someone well acquainted with the patient's circumstances was also required to attend this meeting, to supply further details. If the case was considered suitable and there was a vacancy, the patient was brought before the committee the following week for admission. Shown here is the petition for the admission to Bethlem of Mary Turner, mother of the painter J.M.W. Turner. It was presented by her brother-in-law Joshua Turner.

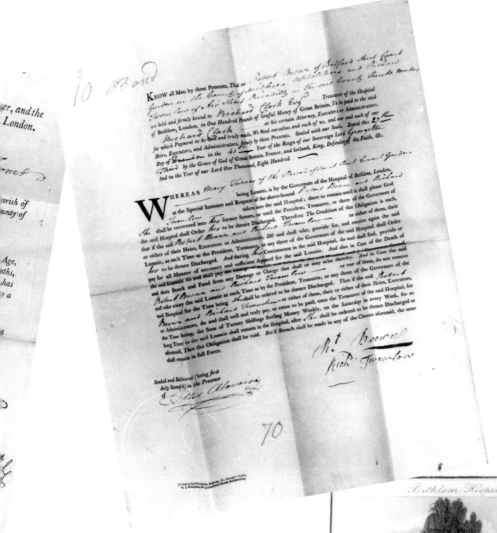

Bethlem Hospital

61 (above right) *Bond relating to the admission of a patient, 1800*
Before a patient could be admitted two house-holders in London or the suburbs had to stand security, and enter into a bond with a penalty of £100. They undertook to pay for the patient's clothing (and at various times, certain other expenses) while in the hospital, and to take him or her away when discharged or pay any funeral expenses. The bond shown here also relates to the admission of Mary Turner. (Mary Turner was transferred to the 'incurable' department after a year in the hospital, where she died in 1804.)

62 *Cries of London, 'Cats and Dogs Meat'*
This series of 'Cries of London' features famous buildings in the background. Here Bethlem's distinctive gateposts, and the eastern pavilion with its balcony and turret, can be seen. The ground has been levelled by this time, and there are no longer steps up to the gates.

CAT'S & DOG'S MEAT!

PORTRAIT OF WILLIAM NORRIS,

SKETCHED FROM THE LIFE, BY G. ARNOLD, A.R.A, ON THE SECOND OF MAY, 1814, WHEN HE WAS VISITED BY

C. C. WESTERN, Esq. M.P. Messrs. ROBERT CALVERT, JAMES BEVANS, EDWARD WAKEFIELD, FRANCIS PLACE, Sen. AND FRANCIS PLACE, Jun.

This unfortunate Man was confined about Twelve Years, in the Manner represented in this Engraving, in Bethlem Hospital. Of which Hospital Dr. MUNRO is the Physician, and Mr. JOHN HASLAM the Apothecary.

EXTRACTS relating to WILLIAM NORRIS, taken from the Minutes of Evidence before the COMMITTEE of the Hon. the House of COMMONS on MADHOUSES, in 1815.

EDWARD WAKEFIELD, Esq.
"William Norris stated himself to he 55 years of age, and that he had been confined about 14 years. He was confined by a stout iron ring, rivetted round his neck, from which a short chain passed to a ring, made to slide upwards or downwards on an upright massive iron bar, more than six feet high, inserted into the wall. Round his body a strong iron bar, about two inches wide, was rivetted; on each side the bar was a circular projection, which being fashioned to and inclosing each of his arms, pinioned them close to his sides. This waist bar was secured by two similar bars, which, passing over his shoulders, were rivetted to the waist bar, both before and behind. The iron ring round his neck was connected to the bars on his shoulders by a double link. From each of these bars another short chain passed to the ring on the upright iron bar. We were informed, he was enabled to raise himself, so as to stand against the wall, on the pillow of his bed in the trough bed in which he lay; but it is impossible for him to advance from the wall in which the iron bar is soldered, on account of the shortness of his chains, which were only TWELVE INCHES LONG. It was, I conceive, equally out of his power to repose in any other position than on his back. The projections which on each side of the waist-bar inclosed his arms, rendering it impossible for him to lie on his side, even if the length of the chain from his neck and shoulders would have permitted it. His right leg was chained to the trough in which he had remained, THUS encaged and chained, MORE THAN 12 YEARS."

WM. SMITH, Esq. M.P.
"I was informed that he had been chained down in his wooden bedstead for above nine years, which did then, and has ever since appeared to me, as a most rigorous and unnecessarily cruel mode of restraint. The cruel and constant coercion in which he was kept, and which, when continued unremittingly for such a length of time, I should think far better calculated to drive away the reason of a sane man, than to restore a madman to his senses."

C.C. WESTERN, Esq. M.P.
"The description of the irons in which Norris was incased is perfectly correct. At the time I saw Norris, it was impossible to believe the continuance of all his irons was in any degree necessary, if they ever were so."

THE HON. H.G. BENNETT, M.P.
"From what I have seen of various manners in other Hospitals, and places of confinement, I should have no hesitation in saying, that it was a mode of restraint unnecessary and unwarranted. It has always appeared to me, from what I have seen of Bethlem, that the restraint was used THERE more from feelings of revenge, than for purposes of medical care."

MR. JOHN HASLAM.
The drawing from which the above Portrait has been etched, being shewn by the Committee to Mr. Haslam, he was asked—"Do you admit it as a correct representation of the manner in which Norris was confined?"—he replied,
"I think the apparatus is all correct."
Being asked the reason for the multiplied means of restraint contrived for Norris, he answered,
"I can give no reason for the contrivance at all, not having contrived it."

WILLIAM NORRIS.

"Standing Rules and Orders for the GOVERNMENT of the Royal Hospitals of Bridewell and Bethlem, with the DUTY OF THE GOVERNORS, and of the several OFFICERS AND SERVANTS.

"GENERAL ORDERS, 8th Clause.——No Patient is to be confined in Chains without the previous Knowledge and Approbation of the Apothecary, nor released from such Confinement without his Consent.

"The Bethlem Sub-Committee is to view the House and Patients at least once a Month, and to minute down any thing of moment in a Book."

NORRIS IS DEAD.

PRINTED BY J. M'CREERY, BLACK-HORSE-COURT, FLEET-STREET, LONDON, AND PUBLISHED BY G. ARNOLD, No. 2, WESTON STREET, PENTONVILLE.

1815.

63 *James* [sic] *Norris, in the iron apparatus in which he was restrained for ten years*
James Norris's case became a *cause célèbre* during the 1815 parliamentary enquiry into madhouses (*see* p.42). (Unfortunately his name was published in the report, as in this broadsheet, as 'William'.) An American seaman, he was exceptionally violent and dangerous when first admitted, and made murderous attacks on fellow patients and staff. He could not be restrained by conventional manacles because his wrists were larger than his hands, enabling him to slip them off and use them as weapons. He was 'discovered' in Bethlem in 1814 in the iron harness shown here, which pinioned his arms: a chain from the iron collar round his neck allowed him to move only as far as the edge of his bed. He had been restrained like this since 1804. He was freed from the irons shortly before his death in 1814.

64 *Manacles and leg irons*
Norris's case was uniquely horrendous, but a lesser degree of physical restraint with irons and chains was a standard part of Bethlem's regime at this time. Patients were regularly chained to the wall during the day, as well as to their beds at night.

Unfortunately the governors' pride in their palatial new building turned out to have been seriously misplaced. The land on which it stood had originally been a section of the old City ditch, filled up without much thought for what was eventually to go on top of it. The building, as revealed by an exhaustive survey carried out in 1799, was virtually without foundations, and had been badly constructed of poor materials, 'hurried and put together, with inconsiderate zeal; and more haste than provident wisdom'. Weighed down by massive roofs and with the infill of the ditch settling under it, it had lasted scarcely a century before there was 'not one of the floors which are level, nor any of the walls upright', and the walls were actually separating from each other at the corners with little to hold them together. The final condemnation of a building which had been celebrated in its heyday for being so airy and light, was that it was 'dreary, low, melancholy, and not well aired'.

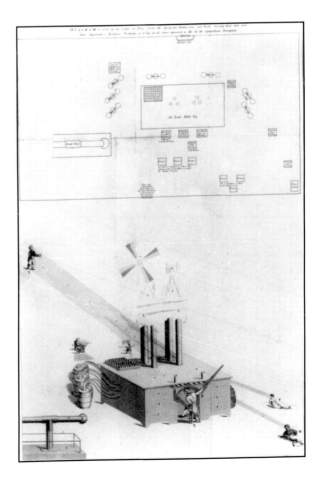

65 *James Tilly Matthews: drawing of an 'Air Loom',* c.*1810*
This is Matthews's diagram of the 'Air Loom', a machine by means of which he believed that he was being 'assailed' by a gang of seven people who included Jack the Schoolmaster, Sir Archy, and the Glove Woman. 'Magnetic fluid' played a large part in the Air Loom's operation, and among the tortures which were practised on him by the gang were 'lobster cracking', 'bomb bursting' and 'lengthening the brain'. Matthews had been confined in Bethlem in 1797, on the considerable evidence of his own writings that he suffered from paranoid delusions. He was believed to be a danger to members of the government and the royal family. His relatives made several attempts to get him released, bringing in physicians to declare him sane. In response John Haslam, the apothecary of Bethlem, published *Illustrations of Madness* in 1810, in which Matthews's enormously complicated delusional system was expounded, largely in his own words, and the drawing of the Air Loom was reproduced.

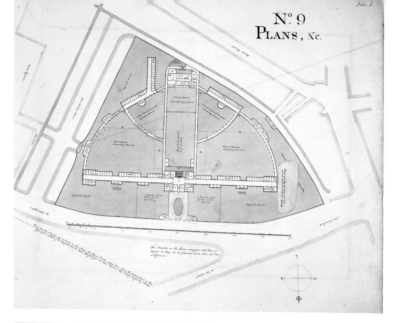

66 *James Tilly Matthews: proposed plan for the new Bethlem Hospital*
Matthews, a tea dealer by trade, showed considerable talent for architectural drawing while he was in Bethlem. In 1810 he submitted his own plans for the competition to design the new hospital, for which the governors awarded him an *ex gratia* payment of £30. These plans were returned to his family, but Matthews continued to submit further plans (from which these examples are taken), together with volumes of meticulous explanation, in an effort to influence the architect James Lewis in his design of the hospital. The drawing illustrated here shows the general layout proposed by Matthews, which interestingly includes the oval front lawn which did eventually become part of the hospital's garden.

67 *James Tilly Matthews: proposed elevations for Bethlem Hospital*

68 *James Tilly Matthews: proposed plan for the upper floor of Bethlem Hospital*

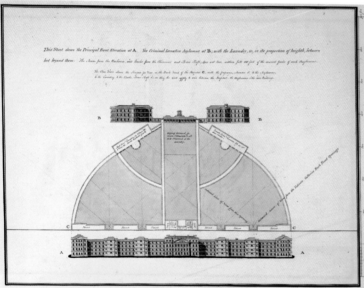

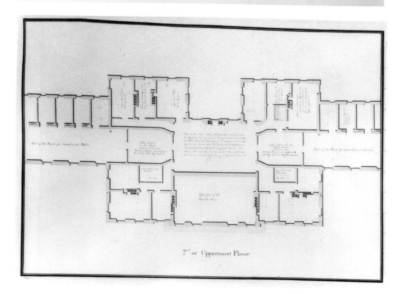

By 1805 it had become necessary to demolish the east wing, while the search began for a new site on which to start again. The Moorfields lease proved a handicap because of its clause requiring that a hospital be kept standing there, and the problem was eventually solved by the governors receiving a parcel of land at St George's Fields in Southwark by way of exchange. (An earlier intention had been to move to Islington.) The new site was to be held for the remainder of the 999-year term of the 1674 lease. In 1810 a competition was held to design a new building, and three premiums were awarded, but the final design was by the hospital's surveyor James Lewis.

In the meantime conditions in the old hospital had deteriorated badly. Ironically the end of public visiting probably led to worse abuses, since the patients were now left

69 *Bethlem Hospital as it appeared in 1811*
This picture, though engraved for *The Beauties of England and Wales*, shows Bethlem in decline. The eastern end of the building has already been demolished; the pineapples appear to have gone from the front wall, and the lion and unicorn from the lower gate piers. Even Moorfields itself is looking rather tired, its neat trees overgrown, its fences broken down, and children sailing boats on a pond where none was intended to be.

to the mercy of their attendants behind closed doors, and the attendants no longer had either the diversion of showing visitors around, or the encouragement of tips arising from it. The dilapidated state of the building itself, the uncertainty about its future, and the preoccupation with moving made matters worse after the turn of the century, and the governors gave little attention to supervising or inspecting the hospital for months on end. An appalling picture of neglect and misery emerges, from the evidence published in 1815 by a Parliamentary Committee which enquired into the state of madhouses in England. This harrowing report should not, however, be taken as representing conditions at all previous times: it almost certainly shows Bethlem at its lowest ebb.

70 *'Bethlehem's Beauty, London's Charity and the City's Glory'—to be taken down and cleared away by the purchasers*
The days of Bethlem's glory ended ignominiously when the fabric was sold off for building materials. This catalogue of the final three days' sale includes 'the highly esteemed North Entrance Gates, and Stone Piers, ornamented with Ionic Columns, Scroll Pediments, and other corresponding Dressings, well calculated for embellishing a Park Entrance, at a small Expence', as well as the stone-fronted central elevation whose 'grace and ornament' had once been the pride of the City of London.

71 *Lots 223 and 224*
It is recorded in the catalogue that Lot 223, the ornate Portland stone front of the central pavilion, with rustic basement, corinthian pilasters and entablature, and semi-circular pediment filled with the royal arms whose 'spaceousness' had caused the governors such heart searching, was sold for £53. Lot 224, the 'highly esteemed' gates, including the piers and pediments on which Raving and Melancholy Madness had lately rested, made £28. (It is possible that there is still a gentleman's residence somewhere in the countryside whose park entrance is embellished by the gates of Bedlam.)

Valuable Building Materials,
Bethlem Hospital, Moorfields.

A
CATALOGUE
OF THE LAST PORTION OF THE VERY DESIRABLE
MATERIALS,
OF BETHLEM HOSPITAL,
Comprised in the remaining part of the East and West Gallery and the center Building.

(To be taken down and cleared away by the Purchasers.)

WHICH WILL BE
Sold by Auction,
BY ORDER OF THE GOVERNORS,

By Mr. UPTON,

On the PREMISES, on MONDAY, March 25, 1816, And Two following Days, at TWELVE O'CLOCK,

All the remaining valuable Materials and Fixtures contained in that Portion of the Building late the Residence of the Officers and Establishment;—Also the highly esteemed North Entrance Gates, and Stone Piers, ornamented with Ionic Columns, Scroll Pediments, and other corresponding Dressings, well calculated for embellishing a Park Entrance, at a small Expence.

The Buildings comprise a quantity of Sound Bricks, Leadwork, Oak, and Fir Timber, in Roofs, Floors, and Partitions; Clean and Common Deal Floor Boards; real Wainscot Doors, Wainscottings, Mouldings, and Stairs; also Deal Wainscottings, Staircases, Sashes, Frames, Shutters, Linings, Doors, Dressers, Shelves, Partitions, &c.; a Stone-fronted Elevation, with Corinthian Entablatures, Pilasters, Circular Pediments, Ashlerings, Architraves, &c. The Stone Ionic Columns, Entablatures, and Dressings at the South Entrance Doorway, of modern Execution, and reconvertible for a similar Purpose, at a moderate Expence; also a great Portion of Stone Paving, a small ditto of Pantiling and Westmorland Slating, several Stone and Lead Sinks, Lead Cisterns, Kitchen-Ranges, Smoke Jacks, some useful Ironwork, and numerous Articles, adapted to the various Purposes of Repairs or Building.

To be viewed on SATURDAY preceding the Sale, with Catalogues (Price Six-pence each, to be allowed to purchasers) which may be had on the Premises, and of Mr. UPTON, adjoining New Bethlem Hospital, St. George's Fields.

III

St George's Fields

1815-1930

'New Bethlem' was opened in August 1815 for 200 patients, with a plan which was heavily dependent on that of its predecessor. The front was 580 feet long, and again the wards consisted of galleries with individual sleeping rooms opening off one side. This time, however, they were on four stories, and were separated by a central area containing committee rooms, offices, residences for certain key officers, and a room where patients could see their visitors. With a larger number of smaller wards, a better 'classification' of patients was hoped for.

In two independent blocks at the back, the new State Criminal Lunatic Asylum was housed. Built and maintained entirely at government expense and controlled by the Home Office, this department was physically attached to Bethlem and run by the hospital authorities on a day-to-day basis. It remained at Bethlem

72 *Silver trowel, hallmarked 1811*
This trowel was used to lay the foundation stone of the third Bethlem Hospital on Saturday 18 April 1812. The engraved inscription lists all the principal people present including the president Sir Richard Carr Glyn (who wielded the trowel), the treasurer Richard Clark, the Lord Mayor, sheriffs and aldermen of the City of London and the governors of the hospital. James Lewis, architect, and Richard Upton, superintendent of works, are also named. On the back are engraved the arms of Bethlem and of Sir Richard Carr Glyn.

from its opening in 1816 until replaced by a new institution at Broadmoor in Berkshire in 1864.

The main building cost just over £122,000, of which more than half came from parliamentary grants and some from a public appeal. In these circumstances lavish ornamentation, in the manner of the Moorfields building, would not have been prudent. The main decorative feature was a massive and rather gloomy portico in the ionic style, remote in spirit from the Moorfields corinthian and innocent of swags, wreaths, fruit or other frivolities. Even the royal arms in the centre of the pediment was subject to an economy drive, and was made of Messrs. Coade and Sealey's artificial stone at a fraction of the cost of quarried stone. A small pumpkin-shaped cupola was all that crowned the squat central lantern, to be replaced 30 years later by Sydney Smirke's far prettier, though probably not (to purists) very correct, dome. Extensions to the building were made at around the same time to accommodate a further 166 patients.

If the outside was more austere, the inside was appropriately less so. The windows of the sleeping rooms were glazed—though only as an afterthought—and a rudimentary central heating system warmed at least the lower parts of the building. The keeper's room on each ward had a fireplace with a protective iron cage, where a 'comfortable fire' was always kept except in hot weather. The more orderly patients had access to these rooms for use as sitting rooms, when not at work or out of doors in the airing courts. There were also separate 'day rooms' doubling as dining rooms. Basic bedding was a stump iron bedstead with a canvas stretcher, flock bed, sheets, blankets, and a rug and bolster. Only in the basement was straw still regularly used for bedding, and physical restraint was considerably reduced.

73 *Ground plan and elevation of the third Bethlem Hospital*
It can be seen from this plan and elevation how closely the layout of the new building followed that of the old, with long galleries and sleeping cells opening off them. The beginnings of two further wings at the back project at right angles to the main galleries. These were to be extended when more money should become available, and were completed in the late 1830s. In the criminal wing for men (top right of the plan) the galleries were dark and oppressive, with bedrooms on both sides and only a single window at each end.

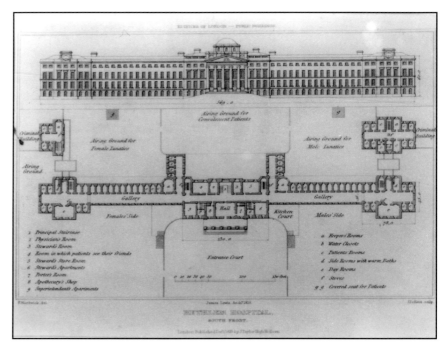

74 *New Bethlem Hospital, St George's Fields, as it appeared when it was opened in 1815*
This picture by Thomas Shepherd shows the third Bethlem as it appeared for twenty years after it was opened. When the line of the road was altered in the 1830s the governors acquired more land at the front, enabling them to move the wall and lay out ornamental gardens with the distinctive oval lawn which still exists today.

75 *Dr. Edward Thomas Monro, physician to Bethlem Hospital 1816-1853: portrait by his son Dr. Henry Monro*
Edward Thomas Monro was not only the last of the Monro dynasty to practise at Bethlem, he was the last holder of the post of visiting physician. He was appointed joint physician in succession to his father, sharing the post with Sir George Tuthill until 1835 and then with Sir Alexander Morison. In 1851 the Commissioners in Lunacy investigated conditions in the hospital. Another critical report followed, and although the findings were not so bad as those of 1815, the governors decided to abolish the post of visiting physician and appoint a full-time resident physician super-intendent. Monro received a pension, and contin-ued to act occasionally as *locum tenens*.

The 'classification' of patients, though better than before, was fairly rough and ready. The basement gallery was for the furious, mischievous, and 'those who have no regard to cleanliness'. The ground floor was for 'ordinary' patients on admission, and those who had been promoted from the basement, and the first floor for convalescents. The incurable wards must originally have been on the top floor.

The provision of occupation for the patients, which had been attempted in the previous buildings, was better organised in the new hospital. Female patients who were able to do so helped around the house, making beds, washing up, and cleaning the galleries. They also worked in the laundry and did all the plain needlework. The men's side had capstans in the airing courts, and male patients pumped all the water needed by the hospital. They were also employed in knitting, tailoring and mending clothes.

10

New House.

The case of Kemp, a patient now in the house, a man of good education, and who has lived in respectable circumstances, who has not only the misfortune of being disordered, but of being poor; on his admittance he was put in Blackburn's gallery, but not suiting him, he contrived to get him removed into the basement by the following means: he (Blackburn) complained to Dr. Tothill (Kemp's physician,) that he of a night made so much noise that he disturbed the other patients and prevented their recovery and got other patients to corroborate his assertion, for this he was removed into the basement, but I know if he had money, or been a good cleaner all would have been well, and he might have remained there, as there are patients who make far more noise now in his gallery; the villain without any provocation had the cruelty to say to Kemp, had *I a dog like you I would hang him.* Another patient named Harris, for the trifling offence of wanting to remain in his room a little longer one morning than usual, was dragged by Blackburn, assisted by Allen, the basement keeper, from No. 18, to Blackburn's room, and there beaten by them unmercifully; when he came out his head was streaming with blood, and Allen in his civil way wished him a good morning.

The case of Morris; this man had some pills to take, which he contrived to secrete in his waistcoat pocket, this Blackburn discovered, and by the assistance of Allen, they got him to his room and there beat him so dreadfully for ten minutes as to leave him totally incapable of moving for some time, Rodbird was looking out to give them notice of the approach of any of the officers; they are three villains. A man of the name of Baccus, nearly eighty years of age, was this summer admitted into the house; one very hot day he had laid down in the green yard, another patient named Lloyd, very much disordered, trod on the middle of his body purposely, this Blackburn the keeper encouraged by laughing, and Lloyd would have repeated it but something diverted his attention: Baccus is since dead.

Coles, a patient of Blackburn's, one day, for refusing to take his physic, was by Blackburn and Rodbird beat and dashed violently against the wall several times, in the presence of the steward, though from the general tenor of this man's conduct it is probable a little persua-

11

sion would have been sufficient to induce him to take the medicine quietly, Coles is since put upon the long list, and is now in the upper gallery.

This keeper has held his situation seven years and from his attention to his business out of the hospital and the care of his birds and his cage making, and his being so much out, his place is almost a sinecure; as to his being out that cannot be without the steward's permission which is too often the case, I will give one instance, this summer the day that Allen the basement keeper was married to a woman keeper, Blackburn was out the whole day, which was Tuesday, the following Thursday after the Committee had left sitting; he again asked the steward to let him go out, but was refused on account of his having five new patients in that day; the next day he went out; I will allow that his gallery is kept very clean, but how is it done? by rousing his patients by five o'clock in a morning, to get all in order that he may attend to his private concerns, which are by far greater objects of solicitude with him than his public duties.

Dowie, keeper of the second gallery.

He has a patient named Clarke, not long since being very much disordered, it was thought necessary to handcuff him; this man was in the habit of picking grass, putting it in his pocket; one day in the green yard, Dowie in my hearing told a patient of the name of Locke if he saw him do amiss to give him a blow or two, Clarke moving to another part of the yard avoided Lock's notice, who seeing another patient act as he thought improperly gave him several violent blows.

Some time ago, Dowie had a patient by trade a tailor who earned money by working for the servants, this man not finding the house allowance sufficient paid Dowie 5s. per week, to let him have as much as he could eat, this would have been fair if Dowie had disposed of what belonged to himself, but instead of that he robbed the other patients of part of their allowance; what honesty!

Mr. Sutherland, a patient under Dowie's care was occasionally visited by his sister, they were too poor to fee Dowie, and the consequence was the following act of inhumanity; one Monday morning while conversing with her brother she fainted (I believe from privation,)

76   The Interior of Bethlehem Hospital, *by Urbane Metcalf, 1818*
This pamphlet was published by a former patient Urbane Metcalf, shortly after his discharge from Bethlem in 1818, in order to expose the cruelties and abuses which he claimed were still being practised in the new hospital. He had also been a patient in old Bethlem for nearly two years in 1804-6, and acknowledged that there had been many improvements, but claimed that the staff ignored the regulations and did as they liked. The pamphlet is an indictment of many named keepers, citing specific episodes of their inhumanity to individual patients. It is difficult to know quite how much to believe, but Metcalf's picture of Bethlem is certainly very different from the one which the governors were at pains to present to the public.

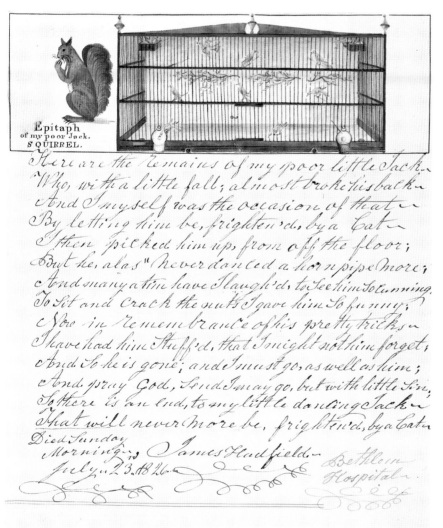

Epitaph
of my poor Jack.
S QUIRREL.

Here are the Remains of my poor little Jack,
Who, with a little fall; almost broke his back,
And I myself was the occasion of that
By letting him be, frighten'd, by a Cat
I then picked him up, from off the floor;
But he, alas" never danced a hornpipe more.
And many a time have I laugh'd, to see him so cunning,
To Sit and Crack the nuts I gave him So funny;
Now in remembrance of his pretty tricks,
I have had him Stuff'd, that I might not him forget,
And So he is gone; and I must go, as well as him;
And I pray God, Send I may go, but with little Sin;
So there is an end, to my little dancing Jack,
That will never more be, frighten'd, by a Cat.
Died Sunday
Morning, James Hadfield, Bethlem
July 23, 1826. Hospital

---

77 *Poem and drawing by James Hadfield*
Hadfield was a patient in the criminal department from 1816 until his death in 1841. His attempt to assassinate King George III in 1800 had set in motion the first criminal lunacy legislation to be passed by parliament, the Act which provided for detention 'until His Majesty's Pleasure shall be known' for those who had been found not guilty by reason of insanity. He became well known to visitors for the pet animals and birds which he kept in his cell, including cats, dogs and a squirrel. He also wrote, illustrated, and sold poems about them, such as the one shown here.

---

78 *James Hadfield's attempt to shoot the King at the Drury Lane Theatre, 1800*
This print follows quite closely the events as they are recorded elsewhere. The king had just entered the royal box, followed by the queen and the princesses. Hadfield was seated two rows from the orchestra and, after he had fired his pistol, some of the musicians assisted in dragging him over the 'pallisade' into the orchestra room. It was later demonstrated at his trial that he had become insane after receiving very severe head injuries while serving in the army.

79 *Bethlem's property at Charing Cross in the 1820s*

Amongst its more valuable endowment estates, Bethlem had possessed a property in the vicinity of Charing Cross since at least 1403. (It has been suggested that insane patients were first transferred to the hospital in Bishopsgate from this property, the Stone House, towards the end of the 14th century.) This picture shows some of the buildings which had developed on the site, shortly before they were all demolished under the Charing Cross improvement scheme. The street frontages were 5-9 Charing Cross and 141-147 St Martin's Lane. The Charing Cross houses and shops are on the left of the picture (two of them occupied at this time by lottery contractors).

80 *Trafalgar Square, site of Bethlem's former possessions*
In 1830 Bethlem was forced to give up its property at Charing Cross, along with other landholders in the area, so that Trafalgar Square could be laid out, and received land and buildings in Piccadilly in exchange. At least one of Landseer's southernmost lions sits on the former Bethlem land.

81 *One of Bethlem's best known tenants*
On the wall beside the lower windows can be seen two of the 19th-century property marks bearing the arms of Bethlem which were put on all the hospital's buildings. Messrs. Richard Fortnum and John Mason became tenants four years after Bethlem received the Piccadilly estate in exchange for its portion of Trafalgar Square. Other early tenants on this estate included the *Cavendish Hotel* (already *in situ*), later to be exploited by Rosa Lewis for not quite respectable purposes, and Hatchard's bookshop.

Jonathan Martin was committed to the criminal department of Bethlem in 1829 after his attempt—nearly successful—to burn down York Minster. A tanner by trade, he had been influenced by prophetic dreams for most of his life, and had spent some time in a private asylum in Northumberland. In the 1820s he took to the road, preaching against the corrupt state of the established church and foretelling the destruction of England by 'the son of Bonaparte'. On receiving no reply to the notes which he addressed to the clergy of York warning them to repent, he reinforced the message by setting fire to the Minster. This is one of the drawings of Bethlem patients which were made to illustrate Sir Alexander Morison's book, *The Physiognomy of Mental Diseases.* (Although dated 1839, the original drawing must have been made earlier since Martin died in 1838.)

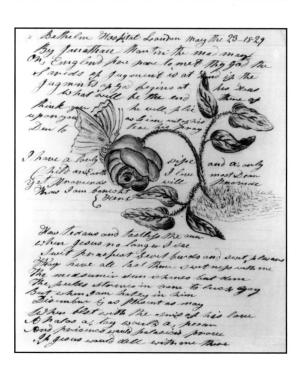

83 (bottom left) *Jonathan Martin, text and drawing, 1829*

Martin's drawings and writings were collected as souvenirs while he was awaiting trial at York, and also when he reached Bethlem. This piece beginning 'Oh England pere pare [prepare] to met thy God', was written within a month of his arrival. The defiant declaration, 'By Jonathan Martin the madman', reflects his annoyance at his family and friends for having arranged for a defence of insanity at his trial. He claimed to have been carrying out God's instructions, and 'God would not have taken a madman to do His work'.

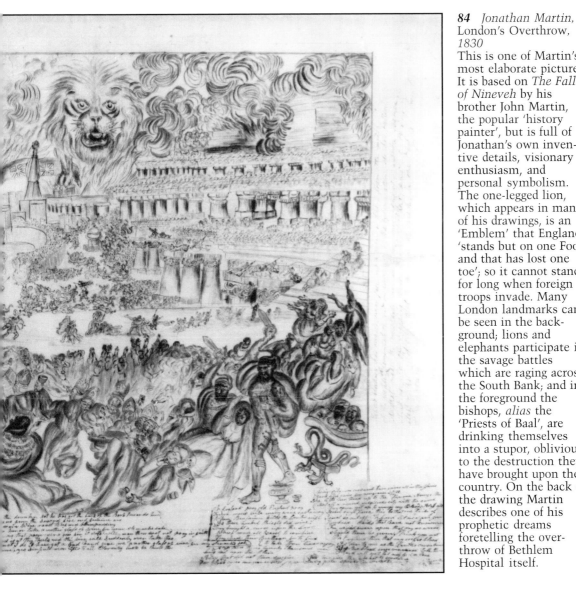

84 *Jonathan Martin, London's Overthrow, 1830*

This is one of Martin's most elaborate pictures. It is based on *The Fall of Nineveh* by his brother John Martin, the popular 'history painter', but is full of Jonathan's own inventive details, visionary enthusiasm, and personal symbolism. The one-legged lion, which appears in many of his drawings, is an 'Emblem' that England 'stands but on one Foot, and that has lost one toe'; so it cannot stand for long when foreign troops invade. Many London landmarks can be seen in the background; lions and elephants participate in the savage battles which are raging across the South Bank; and in the foreground the bishops, *alias* the 'Priests of Baal', are drinking themselves into a stupor, oblivious to the destruction they have brought upon the country. On the back of the drawing Martin describes one of his prophetic dreams foretelling the overthrow of Bethlem Hospital itself.

85 *Instruments of restraint: belt and manacles, as worn by Jonathan Martin*
Not surprisingly, Martin made determined efforts to escape from Bethlem, and was kept under restraint for at least some of the time. In the text which forms part of *London's Overthrow*, he reveals that he drew the picture under the considerable difficulty of having 'a pound of iron on each hand, bound to my loins with seven pounds more …', clearly a description of the sort of device illustrated here.

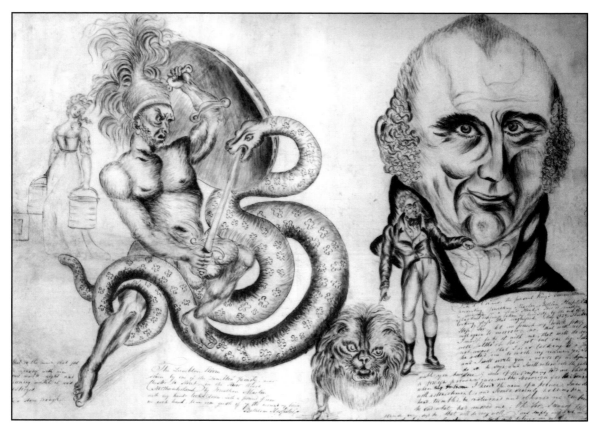

86 *Jonathan Martin,* The Lambton Worm, *with a self portrait and other drawings*
The Lambton Worm was a local legend from Northumberland, where Martin was born, though his representation of it is not quite as the story tells. On the right-hand side is 'Jonathan Martin's likeness taken by himself by the aid of a looking glass that magnified. May 1829.'

87 *Jonathan Martin,* Hell's Gates
This drawing, rather more confused in layout than some of his others, contains many of Martin's favourite themes such as the one-legged lion, a bishop with 'seven heads and ten horns' (though only one head is visible), and other apocalyptic symbolism.

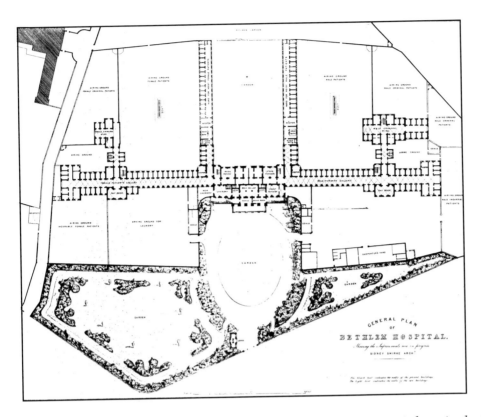

88 (above)   *Ground plan showing extensions and improvements carried out in the 1830s*
This plan shows extensions to the building which were added by Sydney Smirke, including the completion of the two wings at the back, which almost doubled the accommodation. It also shows the new lay-out at the front, made possible by the acquisition of extra land when the road was diverted. The gardens, with their distinctive amoeba-shaped beds filled with shrubs, were designed by Smirke's predecessor Phillip Hardwick, and were planted by the nurserymen Messrs. Rollinson & Son of Tooting for £250. The oval lawn can still be seen in front of the Imperial War Museum, which now occupies what is left of the building.

89 (top right)   *Attempted assassination of Queen Victoria by Edward Oxford, 1840*
In 1840 Edward Oxford, then aged 18, fired two pistols at Queen Victoria as she drove to Hyde Park with Prince Albert. There was some doubt as to whether the pistols were loaded, but Oxford was tried for high treason, and was lucky to be found not guilty by reason of insanity. He was confined in the criminal department at Bethlem for the next 24 years, though consistently reported by the physicians as being 'Sane' in their quarterly returns to the Home Secretary. The most likely explanation for his act seems to be the youthful bravado of a somewhat disturbed adolescent.

90 (right)   *Edward Oxford in Bethlem in the 1850s*
Against all the odds Oxford made good his time in Bethlem, 'devoting all his leisure time to instructive reading and study'. He learnt French, German and Italian, and acquired some Spanish, Latin and Greek. He became an expert house painter and wood grainer and a proficient knitter, excelled at chess and fives, and took up the violin. He was befriended by the steward of the hospital, G.H. Haydon, whose 'many acts of kindness' he later acknowledged. In 1864 he was transferred to the newly built Broadmoor Asylum, from which he was freed three years later on condition that he emigrate. He made a new life for himself in Australia under the evocative name of John Freeman and, 20 years later, sent to Haydon a copy of his recently published *Lights and Shadows of Melbourne Life*, along with some articles for the English papers.

91 (far right)   *Edward Oxford, letter to G.H. Haydon, 27 November 1867*
Two days before his release from Broadmoor, Oxford had written to Haydon at Bethlem thanking him for his past kindness. The note shown here, 'the first independent act of my new existence', was scribbled just before he embarked for Australia: it records how, for the first time for nearly 28 years, he has 'slept ... with the key of the bed-room door on my side'. (National Library of Australia: MS 243)

54

92 *Dr. (William) Charles Hood, physician superintendent of Bethlem 1852-62*
Dr. (later Sir) Charles Hood became the hospital's first resident physician superintendent in 1852, at the age of 28, ending the 125-year rule of the Monro family as visiting physicians. His appointment was part of a programme to reform the hospital, after the unfavourable report by the Lunacy Commissioners. Together with the newly appointed steward George Henry Haydon, another young man of energy and humane outlook, he worked tirelessly to improve conditions for the patients in every aspect of their lives.

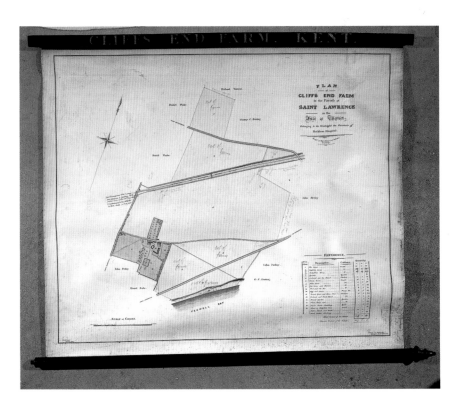

93 *Cliff's End Farm, near Ramsgate, 1853*
Another of the endowment properties, Cliff's End Farm was bequeathed to Bethlem in 1702 and is the only farm still in the hospital's possession. This is one of many beautiful estate plans of Bethlem's properties which were made in the 19th century.

In spite of all its improvements, 'New Bethlem' was still a bleak and comfortless place by modern standards—and even by mid-19th-century ones. The main period of reform came in the 1850s, though even before this the gallery windows were being enlarged, letting in more light and enabling those inside to see out. From 1852 onwards, under the leadership of the young resident physician Dr. (later Sir) Charles Hood, and the steward George Henry Haydon, a programme of transformation was begun. The wards were more comfortably furnished; birds, flowers books, pictures and music were introduced; occupation and recreation was provided both inside and outside the hospital walls; and the status of the attendants was gradually raised to bring them nearer to the modern idea of nurses, and away from that of 'keepers'.

94 *Mrs. Emma Dunn, matron of Bethlem 1854-69*
The post of matron had existed since at least 1630, though originally it was filled by the porter's wife without any extra pay. The matron supervised the work of all the female servants and the care of the female patients, and by the 19th century she had considerable responsibility and authority on the female side of the hospital. Mrs. Dunn is the first matron of whom we have a picture.

95 *Design for a garden, 1854*
Among the improvements carried out around this time, the airing grounds were converted from 'mere bare cheerless enclosures' into pleasant gardens. This drawing shows the architect Sydney Smirke's new design for the main airing ground for male patients.

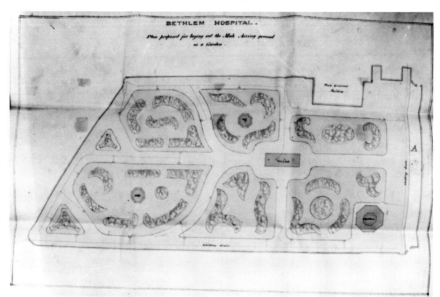

96 *The painter Richard Dadd, a patient in the criminal department 1844-64*

Richard Dadd was committed to the criminal department of Bethlem Hospital when he was 27, after killing his father in the deluded belief that he was killing the devil in disguise. Previously considered to be one of the most talented young artists of his generation, he continued painting and drawing throughout his 20 years of confinement in Bethlem and a further 22 in Broadmoor. He died in Broadmoor in 1886. In this photograph, taken in Bethlem in the 1850s, he is working on one of his two great masterpieces of fairy painting, *Contradiction. Oberon and Titania*. It was painted for the physician superintendent Dr. Charles Hood. (*The Fairy Feller's Master-stroke*, which is now in the Tate Gallery, was painted for the steward G.H. Haydon.) During the 1850s Dadd also worked on a series of watercolours with the overall title 'Sketches to Illustrate the Passions', and many of the pictures which are now in the Bethlem collection are from this series.

97 (left) *Richard Dadd*, Sketch of the Passions. Hatred, *1853*
This picture is sub-titled 'Murder of Henry 6th by Richard Duke of Gloster. See how my sword weeps the poor king's death.' Dadd had stabbed his father to death, and there can be little doubt that he identified closely with the scene depicted here, though on the whole he rarely portrayed the violence which he occasionally felt impelled to enact.

98 (centre) *Richard Dadd*, Sketch to Illustrate the Passions. Agony—Raving Madness, *1854*
Though Dadd was surrounded by models from whom he could have realistically portrayed 'raving madness', he chose never to do so. For this study he has opted for the standard stereotype of a chained lunatic lying on straw, in a scene which had long since ceased to exist in Bethlem.

99 (right) *Richard Dadd*, Sketch to Illustrate the Passions. Insignificance or Self Contempt, *1854*
The figure in this picture is a caricature of J.M.W. Turner, whom Dadd would have remembered from his own student days at the Royal Academy Schools.

100 *Richard Dadd,* Sketch to Illustrate the Passions. Self Conceit or Vanity, *1854*

101 *Richard Dadd,* Sketch to Illustrate the Passions. Grief or Sorrow, *1854*

102 *Richard Dadd*, Sketch of an Idea for Crazy Jane, *1855*
This subject is taken from the popular ballad 'Poor Crazy Jane', which tells the story of a girl driven mad by the desertion of her faithless lover.

103 *Richard Dadd*, A Wayside Inn, *1871*
This delicate little scene was painted after Dadd had been moved to Broadmoor, though at Bethlem he also worked in the very fine stippling technique used here. It is in its original frame, and seems to have been painted specifically for it. Dadd's extraordinary visual memory, and his determination to survive as the artist he had once been, is seen in his continuing ability to paint naturalistic landscape scenes after nearly thirty years' imprisonment.

Photographs of patients taken in the 1850s

For most of its history Bethlem has taken its patients principally from the ranks of the very poor. With a few notable exceptions, little is known about most of them beyond their names and places of origin, which have been recorded in admission registers ever since 1683. Even the more detailed case books, beginning in the early 19th century, at first tell only the broad outline of their brief and troubled passage through the hospital. However, a remarkable series of photographs taken in the mid-1850s adds an extra dimension to the bare administrative and clinical record. For the first time we encounter some of Bethlem's patients as real people with a real physical presence.

104 *A father and son, patients in the hospital at the same time, both suffering from 'melancholia'*

105 *A young woman photographed while suffering from 'puerperal mania'*

106 *The same patient, convalescent*

62

107 *A young woman suffering from 'acute mania'*

108 *The same patient, convalescent*

109 *'Trial Bhethlehem'* [sic] *by Angus Mackay*
This is possibly the only pipe music ever composed in Bethlem. Angus Mackay was Queen Victoria's first household piper, appointed in 1843. An exceptionally talented musician, he was also skilled in writing down the music in staff notation (a recent development, the tunes having traditionally been passed on by ear) and had published a seminal book, *A Collection of Ancient Piobaireachd or Highland Pipe Music*. In 1854 he suddenly became insane and was admitted to Bethlem where, in between episodes of extreme violence and incoherence, he played the pipes, wrote out a volume of tunes, and kept a diary in Gaelic. Most of the tunes were traditional, but 'Triall Bhethlehem' or 'Agmen Bethlehemicum' (Bethlem March) seems to be his own composition. (Mackay was eventually transferred to Crichton Hospital in Dumfries, from which he escaped three years later and was drowned while trying to cross the River Nith.) (National Library of Scotland: Seaforth MS.)

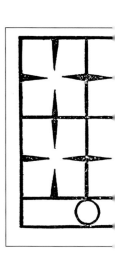

110 (left) *Bethlem in the 1850s*
This watercolour by an unknown artist shows Bethlem at its most pleasant, bathed in golden sunlight and softened by the trees and shrubs of its front garden. In reality, and in most weathers, it must have presented a rather more forbidding appearance. The well-known dome was added in 1844/5 by the hospital's architect Sydney Smirke, who also designed the dome for the British Museum reading room. It housed the chapel. (The present dome of the Imperial War Museum is a reconstruction, the original having been destroyed in an arson attack in 1968.) A descendent of Dr. Charles Hood has identified the figures as being Hood and one of his sons.

111 (below left) *A men's ward in 1860*
This and the companion picture of a women's ward are the first authentic views of the interior of Bethlem since Hogarth's *Rake's Progress* scene of 1735. They appeared in the *Illustrated London News* for March 1860, together with an article about the hospital, and show many of the innovations which had recently been introduced into the wards such as aviaries, plants, pictures, statuary, pet animals, and more comfortable furniture. The patients are occupied as far as possible, and those who are not can at least look out of the windows, which in earlier days had been high in the walls and laden with black painted iron bars.

112 (below centre) *The ironwork which originally secured the windows*

113 (below right) *A women's ward in 1860*
Halfway down this gallery (as in the previous picture) can be seen a large aviary, of which there was one in each ward. It is described in the accompanying article as 'a complete aviary full of joyously-caroling birds; and these little songsters seem to possess much power in raising the sometimes drooping spirits and soothing the troubled minds of the unhappy persons who dwell here'. Individual bird cages and goldfish bowls can be seen hanging by the windows, and the newly invented 'ward cases' for growing ferns stand on the windowsills.

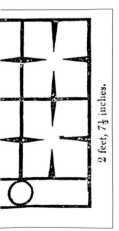

2 feet, 7¼ inches.

The character of the hospital was irrevocably changed with the decision in 1857 to stop admitting 'parish' patients, now that every county must provide its own pauper lunatic asylum. Bethlem remained a charitable hospital for the poor, but preference was to be given to the poor of the middle classes. The last of the criminal patients were transferred to Broadmoor in 1864, and the criminal wings demolished, marking another step towards middle-class respectability. In 1882 a handful of paying patients was admitted for the first time. The numbers gradually increased over the following decades, though a graduated scale of charges according to means still operated, and the 'free list' was never wholly abandoned. Nevertheless, by the time the hospital moved to Monks Orchard in 1930 the prospectus was aimed at 'ladies and gentlemen ... of suitable educational status', a far cry from the 'poor lunatics' who had been Bethlem's charitable objects for most of its history.

114 *A drawing by G.H. Haydon, steward of Bethlem 1853-89*
George Henry Haydon, the kindly, genial and humane steward who shared with Dr. Hood and his successors the task of improving conditions in Bethlem, was originally apprenticed to an architect, and had spent five years in Australia as a very young man. He was a talented and irrepressible artist whose little sketches frequently enlivened his letters and notes to friends and colleagues, as well as, occasionally, the pages of *Punch*. This drawing (date unknown) represents Haydon's version of one of his own predecessors in the post of steward, the 'manciple' of Bethlem.

115 *The convalescent establishment at Witley, Surrey*
Attempts in the mid-19th century to persuade the Bethlem governors to move the hospital out of town were resisted, but in 1870 a convalescent home was opened at Witley in Surrey. The boys' section of King Edward's School (Bridewell Hospital) had already moved here. The building was in the school grounds, and is now a part of the school itself. Patients went for a trial period at Witley before their discharge, the country atmosphere and more relaxed regime helping them to readjust from institutional life. These features were also popular with the staff, and a ward in the present hospital is named 'Witley' in memory of the happy associations with this place.

116 (right) *Supper menu, 1882*
A joke menu issued by G.H. Haydon, 'Maunciple', for a dinner at the hospital.

117 (below) *The Bethlem dance scene in the 1880s*
Rather surprisingly, dances had been held in Bethlem from at least the 1850s, in a large glass-sided ballroom on the top floor of one of the wings at the back. This cartoon from *Punch* suggests that, by the end of the century, a ball at Bethlem was all part of the social season.

118 (below right) *A dance card, 1886*

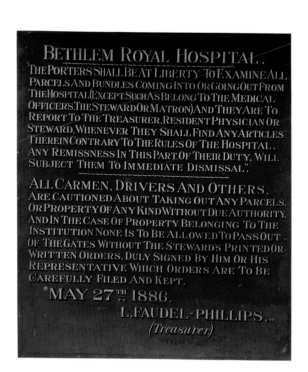

BETHLEM ROYAL HOSPITAL.
"THE PORTERS SHALL BE AT LIBERTY TO EXAMINE ALL
PARCELS AND BUNDLES COMING INTO OR GOING OUT FROM
THE HOSPITAL (EXCEPT SUCH AS BELONG TO THE MEDICAL
OFFICERS, THE STEWARD OR MATRON) AND THEY ARE TO
REPORT TO THE TREASURER, RESIDENT PHYSICIAN OR
STEWARD, WHENEVER THEY SHALL FIND ANY ARTICLES
THEREIN CONTRARY TO THE RULES OF THE HOSPITAL.
ANY REMISSNESS IN THIS PART OF THEIR DUTY, WILL
SUBJECT THEM TO IMMEDIATE DISMISSAL."

ALL CARMEN, DRIVERS AND OTHERS,
ARE CAUTIONED ABOUT TAKING OUT ANY PARCELS,
OR PROPERTY OF ANY KIND WITHOUT DUE AUTHORITY,
AND IN THE CASE OF PROPERTY BELONGING TO THE
INSTITUTION NONE IS TO BE ALLOWED TO PASS OUT
OF THE GATES WITHOUT THE STEWARD'S PRINTED OR
WRITTEN ORDERS, DULY SIGNED BY HIM OR HIS
REPRESENTATIVE WHICH ORDERS ARE TO BE
CAREFULLY FILED AND KEPT.
MAY 27TH 1886.
L. FAUDEL-PHILLIPS.
(Treasurer)

119 *Painted notice board from the porter's lodge*

120 *The front gates and porter's lodge, 1912*

The second half of the 19th century saw the wards growing ever more luxurious, and increasing provisions for occupation and entertainment. Flower gardens were laid out, a recreation hall with fully-equipped theatre was built, electric lighting installed, and the heating system improved, a hospital band flourished, tennis courts were set up, and civilised meals were served in a well lit dining hall. In the early part of this century it would have been easy to assume that Bethlem was an expensive private hospital, rather than the charitable institution which it at least partially remained. Treatment also progressed, and an X-ray department was opened in 1920 followed by a new operating theatre. An outpatients department and medical school were among other innovations in the 1920s.

121 *The chapel in the dome*
Despite its origins as a religious house, Bethlem made little provision for the spiritual welfare of its patients for many centuries. The chaplain of Bridewell attended the Bethlem patients for a brief period in the late 17th/early 18th centuries, but this practice soon ceased. From 1825, a room under the original low cupola was used as a chapel, and finally Smirke's dome replaced this to accommodate the much larger chapel which is seen here, with space for 220 people.

123 *A women's ward at the end of the 19th century*
The size of the windows shows that this ward was on
the top floor, presumably the one known as F4. The
aviaries have gone by this time, the singing birds replaced by the rather less cheerful dead variety in glass
cases, but many more pieces of elegant furniture and
decorative objects have come in. The furnishings now
look like those of a typical comfortable middle-class late
Victorian home, though the uncompromising lay-out
never allowed the Bethlem galleries to look exactly cosy.
A little way down the right-hand wall is a handsome
mahogany buffet with distinctive lyre-shaped supports,
one of relatively few pieces of furniture from this period
to have survived.

124 *The mahogany buffet seen above.*

125 *Pantomime programme, 1897*
A new recreation hall with well equipped stage and dressing rooms was opened in 1896, and outside companies performed comedies there every fortnight. It was also used for dances and home-grown entertainments, such as this performance of *Ali Baba* by members of the hospital staff augmented by their families.

BETHLEM ROYAL HOSPITAL.

❧ PROGRAMME. ❧

. . . MARCH 19th, 1897 . . .

EXTRAORDINARY REVIVAL OF THE AGED AND SENILE EXTRAVAGANZA

❧ "ALI BABA." ❧

And his 40 Thieves, 38 of whom are doing duty on Pirate Omnibuses.

❧ DRAMATIS PERSONÆ. ❧

ALI BABA (*A poor but dishonest Woodcutter*)	DR. M. CRAIG.
GANEM (*His Son, a chip off the old block*)	MR. F. BURNSIDE.
CASSIM BABA (*A rich Merchant of the Baba blacksheep order who in attempting to fleece others gets fleeced himself*)	MR. N. C. CRAIG.
HASSARAC (*The Captain of the Forty, who acts with great forti-tude—a marticet*)	MR. A. H. MARTIN.
ALI BEN ZOUALEN (*A thief, penny plain*)	MR. B. ALCOCK.
ABDULHER (*Another, twopence coloured*)	MR. G. G. CRAIG.
CONBA BABA (*Cassim's larger half, an optical delusion and a regular Persian Cat*)	DR. H. W. B. STODDART.
MORGIANA (*A slave to Ali and circumstance*)	MRS. ARMSTRONG.
ASS (*An ass-tonishing quadruped*)	DR. H. R. PRING.
THIEVES, RUFFIANS, RAG, TAG, BOBTAIL, AND OTHER GENTLEMEN	DR. G. H. GOLDSMITH. MR. P. C. BATES. DR. H. R. PRING.
DANCING GIRLS, SINGING GIRLS AND OTHER GIRLS	MRS. A. H. MARTIN. MISS LALA DI TEGNONE. MISS ISABEL FIELD COLLIER.
AN ENGLISH TOURIST (*Astray from his Band*)	DR. R. PERCY SMITH.

❧ SYNOPSIS OF SCENERY. ❧

Scene 1.—Somewhere in Bagdad.
" 2.—Somewhere out of Bagdad.
" 3.—Entrance to the Robbers' Cave.
" 4.—Ali Baba's Kitchen.

Scene 5.—Interior of the Cave.
At the conclusion of this Scene a marvellous unheard of effect will be revealed by means of an entirely original offer-dip trap. If it—Ali—is set clap-trap. A point will be offered for.
" 6.—Ali's New Palace.

Incidental Music by the Bethlem Band.
Wigs specially selected and supplied by Mr. C. Holz, of Wellington St., Strand.
The Drop Curtain has been provided with new cords, and the Orchestra have sworn to avoid old chords, lost chords and discords. "Herr Carl Wilhelm is trying to sew that they do so."
Mr. A. H. Martin has, from time to time, endeavoured to act his Stage Manages, but nearly everyone has had his own say.
Scenes I. and VI. and the rock piece in Scene III. have been specially painted and presented by Mr. A. Wallis, of Shepherd's Bush, W., who has also kindly lent Scenes II. and IV.
There will be an interval between Scenes IV. and V. and Scenes V. and VI., the length of which will depend on the activity of the Scene Shifters.
Children in arms and unaccompanied will not be admitted.

126 *A women's ward at the beginning of the present century*
This is ward F3, renamed Victoria in 1904 when all the wards were given names instead of numbers. The furnishings did not change much after the late 19th century, but the fact that electric lighting has been installed (though the gas fittings are still there) helps to date this photograph as being a little later.

127 (left) *19th-century card table*
This little table was rescued from the back of a lorry which was taking it to the hospital bonfire around 1970, shortly before such things came back into fashion. Its companion, which was rather damaged, did not survive. The tables can be seen in several ward photographs from the turn of the century. One or other of them is just visible in the previous photograph of Victoria Ward, standing beyond the open door on the right-hand side.

128 (above) *A men's ward, early 20th century*
This is ward M3, also known as Albert. Though slightly more austere than the women's side, the men's wards contained similar furnishings. A particular feature of the men's galleries, besides the stuffed birds, was a substantial geological collection.

129 (right) *A workroom on the female side,* c.*1905*
The nurse in this picture is staff nurse Maud Whitehead.

The staff fancy dress ball, 1907

130 (above) *Dr. Theophilus B. Hyslop, physician superintendent, as Henry VIII*

131 (left) *Sister Annie Simpson as 'Under the Dome' or Bethlem Hospital*

132 (right) *Miss M.A. Lulham, matron of the convalescent home at Witley, as Night*

133 (below) *Attendant Thomas Leary as a Babe in the Wood*

134 *A game of bowls in the men's airing court*

135 *Croquet on the front lawn*

136 (below) *The hall porter William Gare, c.1910*
William Gare retired because of ill health in 1912, after upwards of
36 years' service. He is carrying the 17th-century porter's staff with
its silver head, and wearing on the sleeve of his cloak one of the
silver badges which seem at one time also to have been worn by the
'basketmen' (ie. male keepers or attendants) of Bethlem. These
regalia were still in use on Founder's Day until the early 1980s.

137 (above right) *The porter's staff with chased silver head, 1682*
The staff head bears the inscription 'The gift of Jno Kendall a
governor of this hospital 1682'. (An entry in the court minutes for
1676 records thanks to Mr. Kendall for the porter's staff, but presumably the head was given later.) It is embossed with acanthus
leaves and the arms of Bethlem, the City of London, the president
Sir William Turner, and the donor. The medallion at the top has the
arms of Henry VIII on one side and of the Stuarts on the other.

138 (right) *The porter's silver badge*
Though hallmarked 1753 the badge has been cast from an earlier
version, and the design probably dates from 1676, when it was
ordered that a badge with the arms of the hospital be provided for
the porter's gown. However, two months earlier it had also been
ordered that 'silver Badges wth. the Armes of the House engraven
thereon' be fastened to the sleeves of the basketmen's coats, and
another identical badge has survived, suggesting that they were all
the same. It is 5° inches high and was probably once enamelled as
the other specimen still is.

139 *Jane, the hospital cat*
The original lantern slide of Jane is sub-titled 'mother of generations'. Her descendents may therefore have been known to, and drawn by, Louis Wain when he was a patient in Bethlem in the 1920s.

140 *Chaplain, chronicler and historian: The Rev. E.G. O'Donoghue*
(Edward) Geoffrey O'Donoghue was chaplain to Bethlem from 1892 until the hospital moved to Monks Orchard in 1930. He was particularly concerned with the welfare and social life of his 'parishioners', and under his editorship the hospital magazine, *Under the Dome*, became a mine of information on social activities and, as he himself would have put it, gossip. In 1914 he published the first (and until this year the only) fullscale history of the hospital, *The Story of Bethlehem Hospital from its foundation in 1247*. It is characteristic that he enlisted the help of several patients in checking, reading and making drawings for this work (tactfully acknowledged in print only as 'friends'). The whimsical, chatty, and occasionally even voyeuristic style of the writing fails to do justice to the indefatigable historical research on which the book is based. Another legacy to subsequent historians is the set of glass lantern slides which he created originally to accompany his historical lectures, but which was continued as a chronicle of contemporary Bethlem life. These have provided many of the illustrations for this book. Appropriately, O'Donoghue is seen here holding the roll of the 1403 Visitation of Bethlem, in the museum of the Public Record Office in Chancery Lane.

141 *Dr. W.H.B. Stoddart, Physician Super-intendent 1910-14*

142 *Dr. Stoddart's parrot*

143 *Col. A.H. Martin, steward of Bethlem 1889-1918*

Bethlem in the 1914-18 War

144 *Garden party for wounded soldiers: the hat trimming competition*
On 28 July 1916 the governors hosted a garden party and concert in the grounds of Bethlem for wounded soldiers from neighbouring military hospitals.

145 *The arrival of the governors at the garden party, loyally greeted by girls from King Edward's School (Bridewell)*

146 *Watching for zeppelins: attendants J.T. Wilson and W. Baldi on the roof*

147 *Produce from the temporary vegetable garden in the front drive*

148 *Attendant C. Ball, tending the supplementary meat ration*

149 *The great bomb crater, 1917*
Two bombs fell in the hospital grounds in September and December 1917, the first causing more damage. Windows were shattered throughout the building, but no one was hurt. The crater presented an irresistible photo-opportunity: Dr. Porter-Phillips takes his turn here.

150 *The recreation hall in use as a temporary dormitory for male patients, after the bombing*

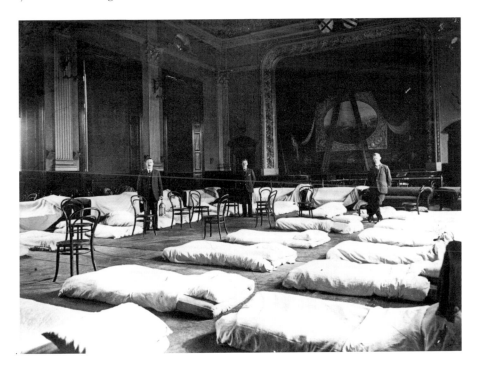

151 *Birthday greetings to Bethlem, 1918*
This drawing is one of many messages received on the hospital's 671st anniversary in 1918, the first occasion for celebration after the return of peace.

152 *The peace procession of 19 July 1919, passing the hospital gates*

The Dog & Duck Club
(1642 – 1924)

The Inaugural Dinner at Oddenino's Restaurant on Friday May 23rd 1924

The President J. G. PORTER PHILLIPS in the Chair

MENU

A face without expression –
MELON

The Chicken Broth – Henry III
The Sorrel Soup

The Lobster – Cardinal Wolsey

The Rib of Lamb with New Peas

The Duck with the Orange Salad

The Old Cream Ice Pudding – Bethlem

The DOG – on Toast

G.L.STAMPA · INVENTIT ET DROODIT May 1924

DOG & DUCK TAVERN

153 *Inaugural dinner of the Dog and Duck Club, 1924*
This dining club for past and present medical officers of Bethlem was named after the somewhat disreputable *Dog and Duck* tavern, which formerly occupied the Bethlem site at St George's Fields. At the top is its stone sign, which was built into one of the hospital walls (now in the Cuming Museum). Holding the dog and duck is Dr. John G. Porter-Phillips, physician superintendent from 1914-44 and founder of the club.

154 (above) *The artist Louis Wain*
Louis Wain was famous from the 1880s onwards
for his cartoon drawings of cats, which remain
popular today. He suffered from a dementia-type
illness towards the end of his life, and was
certified insane in 1924, when in his sixties. He
spent his remaining 15 years in mental hospitals,
including five years in Bethlem from 1925-30. He
died in Napsbury Hospital near St Albans in
1939. He continued drawing and painting almost
to the end, producing brightly coloured land-
scapes and other subjects as well as the cats for
which he was best known.

155 (above) *Louis Wain*, I am Happy because
Everyone Loves Me, c.*1925-30*
This is the sort of picture that Wain would turn
out very rapidly on demand. He never dated his
drawings, but this one belonged to a nurse who
had looked after him at Bethlem, so was presumably drawn during his time in this hospital.

156 (left) *Louis Wain*, The Edge of the Wood
Someone has written 1928 on the back of this
picture, so it may have been painted in Bethlem. It
is, in any case, typical of the colourful pictures
which he produced in both Bethlem and Napsbury.

157   *Louis Wain, drawing in red chalk of a cat*

158   *Louis Wain, Christmas decoration painted on a mirror, 1930s*
Wain first painted a Christmas scene on one of the large mirrors in his ward at Bethlem as part of the
Christmas decorations, and continued the practice when he was transferred to Napsbury. This is one of
the Napsbury mirrors.

Despite its 20th-century innovations, Bethlem remained tied to a late 17th-century lay-out, albeit marginally updated in 1815. Maintenance costs were heavy, and the site was restricted by urban development. Southwark was no longer a healthy environment—or, indeed, a socially suitable one for educated ladies and gentlemen; and the governors and medical staff alike wanted 'light, air and space' and 'ultra modern' facilities. In order to modernise, the hospital would have to move once more, and the search began for a new site in a rural location, but within easy reach of central London.

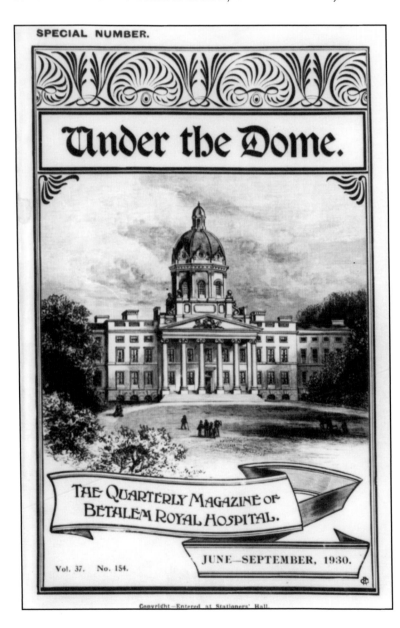

159 Under The Dome: *the end of an era*
The final issue of the hospital's magazine, which had been published since 1892. Fortuitously, the view which was used on the cover represents almost exactly the portion of the building which survives today.

160 *Demolition of the wings of Bethlem*
After the hospital had moved, the site which had
been bought by Lord Rothermere, was given to
the people of Southwark as a public park in
memory of his mother. Much of the building,
including the original galleries, was demolished,
and the remainder was taken over by the Imperial
War Museum.

161 *Opening of the Geraldine Mary
Harmsworth Park*
The new park on the Bethlem site was opened on
12 July 1934. After the opening ceremony, the
guests took a determined stroll round the
grounds.

162 *Monks Orchard House: view across the top lake*
The Monks Orchard Estate, originally called Park Farm and then Wickham Park, acquired its present name in the 1850s, when the owner Lewis Loyd built a new mansion for himself in a part of the estate called Monks Orchard. The house is seen here across one of three ornamental lakes, which were interlinked and reached nearly to the Wickham Road. They were filled in during the 1930s, for safety reasons. They are commemorated in the name of Lake Road nearby.

163 *The drawing room of Monks Orchard House*
The house was originally intended to be kept and used as a nurses' home, but it had stood empty for many years and extensive dry-rot was discovered. It was demolished, and Witley House built on the site.

IV

Monks Orchard

1930-PRESENT

In 1925 the governors bought the Monks Orchard Estate, a country house estate on the Kent/Surrey border comprising 330 acres, of which about ninety were later sold for development. The joint architects of the 250-bed hospital were John Cheston, Bethlem's surveyor, and Charles Elcock, who already had experience in designing hospitals. The plans went through many changes before building started in 1928, most of them dictated by the need to curtail soaring costs. The design was on the 'villa' system, whereby each ward was contained in an independent building with its own garden, while other units housed administration, 'science and treatment laboratories', a chapel, recreation hall, staff restaurant and kitchen, and boiler house and works department. Houses were provided for the senior medical officers, and a separate nurses' home meant that, for the first time in Bethlem's history, the nursing staff had their own accommodation away from the wards.

164 *The terrace of Monks Orchard House* Many features of the gardens surrounding the house survived in the gardens of Witley House until quite recently, including the round bed seen here (but minus the hedges) and many of the paths. Most have now fallen into decay or been removed, but some balustrading can still be found, and much of the ornamental tree planting remains.

The Monks Orchard Estate in the 1920s

165   *Haymaking*

166   *Ploughing*

167 *A rabbit warren*

168 *Pigs at Park Farm*
Park Farm was the home farm of the estate, and
was farmed until 1955. After that the farmhouse
was converted into a residence for male nurses,
but has now been demolished. Market gardening
was continued after the farming ended, and the
pigs were kept until 1959. Those remaining were
sold after an outbreak of swine fever.

169 *The stable block at Park Farm, 1956*
The stables, now demolished, were built about
1828. Described in the 1924 sale brochure as
'model stables', their brick floors were patterned
in herring bone and other decorative designs, and
the partitions to the stalls were filled with
ornamental ironwork. Accommodation for the
grooms was on the left of the arch.

The governors wished their new hospital to be 'magnificent'. More happily, perhaps, the architects settled for 'a simple and dignified effect'. The buildings, faced in small red bricks with artificial stone dressings, make their statement mainly through neat compact design, in a style which was 'modern' at the time but unextreme. The overall look is mildly Georgian, with discreet art deco Egyptian ornamentation, whose subtlety can best be seen in the administration unit. The four wards, after narrowly escaping the 'commonplace and suburban' names of Chestnut, Beech, Pinewood and Broomwood, were named Fitzmary after the hospital's founder; Witley after the former convalescent home at Witley in Surrey; Tyson after Dr. Edward Tyson, a worthy physician to Bethlem from 1684-1708; and Gresham by mistake. (Sir Richard Gresham did not, as was believed, petition Henry VIII for Bethlem on behalf of the City: he notably ignored it when petitioning for several other hospitals.)

170 *The chaplain, the Rev. Geoffrey O'Donoghue, visiting the new site in 1925*

171 *Prince Arthur of Connaught arriving to lay the foundation stone of the new hospital at Monks Orchard, 10 July 1928*
Prince Arthur deputised on this occasion for his father the Duke of Connaught, a governor of the hospital. The foundation stone is in the wall of the administration building, beside the door. It is difficult to understand quite how it got there—or alternatively, where it was laid—since no building work had begun at this stage.

172 *The beginnings of the new hospital, 31 October 1928*
This is one of the earliest of a series of photographs through which the rise of the buildings can be traced month by month. The view here is roughly towards the works department, from the back of Fitzmary House. The foundations of Fitzmary are seen in the bottom left corner, and of Gresham in the centre of the picture. The broad guage railway track was brought in as a branch line from the Southern Railway, at a junction near Eden Park Station, enabling materials to be delivered direct to the site of each building.

173 *The site of the administration building, 31 October 1928*
The view is towards Tyson House, with the stores, kitchen and works department later to appear on the right-hand side.

174 *The foundations of Witley House, 28 June 1929*
This picture shows some of the balustrading and ornamental trees from around Monks Orchard House, which can still be seen today. A small plantation, just behind the trees at the top right-hand corner of the picture, is home to Bethlem's famous badger sett.

175 *The view towards the gate from the administration building, 31 December 1929*
The nearly completed chapel is on the left, and the nurses' home (later Alexandra House) on the right, but Monks Orchard Road has not yet been built. Two trees which now stand on either side of the gate help to identify where it will be, and the roof timbers of the gate lodge can just be seen. The cartwheel-shaped window in the west wall of the chapel was destroyed by bombing in 1944, and has been replaced with a slightly different one.

The research and treatment block was named for the chairman, Lord Wakefield of Hythe, who donated £25,000 towards it. It was considered to be exceptionally well equipped, with an X-ray department, operating theatre, pathology laboratory, and facilities for hydrotherapy, dentistry, psychology and electrical treatment. Lady Wakefield gave £5,000 to save the chapel from economy cuts, and her name was attached to it. Lady Cooper gave a further £5,000 for the recreation hall, to be named the Sir Edward Cooper Recreation Hall in memory of her late husband. Despite generous donations by these and other governors, however, a public appeal for funds proved disappointing, and the final cost of about half a million pounds left the hospital's own resources overstretched for some time to come.

The new hospital was opened in July 1930 by Queen Mary, and occupied in October. Physically, it has changed relatively little since then. The buildings covered only a

small portion of the site, much of which remained as farm and woodland. Today the grounds have something of the character of a nature reserve. Foxes, squirrels, nuthatches, tree creepers and woodpeckers in variety, as well as all the usual garden birds, are every-day sights, while a 30-year-old colony of green parakeets flourishes in the woods. Badgers are often encountered in the evening, and sometimes come to the buildings for food (the author can testify to seeing a badger eating custard cream biscuits within inches of the swimming pool window). In the spring and early summer daffodils and bluebells carpet the ground between silver birches, and the flowering trees and shrubs of the ward gardens remain, though the fences have now gone; but one of the finest visual legacies of the 1930s builders has been the sensitive preservation of existing mature trees amongst and around the new buildings.

176 *Opening of the new hospital, 9 July 1930*
After formally opening the hospital Queen Mary, in pink and blue flowered chiffon and carrying a pink parasol, made an hour-long tour of the buildings in 'blazing sunshine'. Flanked by the president Lord Wakefield of Hythe, the treasurer Sir Lionel Faudel-Phillips, and Dr. Porter-Phillips, she is seen here leading the party back for tea.

177 *The entrance hall of the administration building*

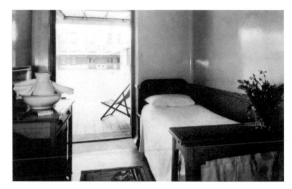

178 *Patients' bedrooms*

179 *The Lady Wakefield Chapel*

180 *The Board Room in the 1930s*
The light fitting and furniture have changed, but the paintings and the arms of the presidents and treasurers still hang round the walls, as they did in previous committee rooms.

181 *The Committee Room in the old hospital at St George's Fields,* c.1910

In every other way, Bethlem has probably seen more change in its last 50 years than in the previous four hundred. In 1948, under the new National Health Service, it was separated from Bridewell and the City of London and united with the Maudsley Hospital in Denmark Hill, Camberwell, to form a single postgraduate psychiatric teaching hospital. Through the Maudsley's far stronger background of teaching and research, unburdened by centuries of tradition, Bethlem was precipitated into a new and faster track. The 'modernity' which everyone had craved in 1930 sent shockwaves through the hospital when it finally struck in 1948, with the physician superintendent and his three medical assistants giving way to a professor of psychiatry, assistant clinical director, and a large staff of senior and junior physicians and registrars, not to mention the newly formed postgraduate Institute of Psychiatry, with another professor already *in situ* and many more to come.

183 (left) *Nursing medal, 1931*
This medal was awarded to nurses at Bethlem on obtaining the certificate in mental nursing from the Royal Medico-Psychological Association, whose training scheme had started in 1890.

184 (top right) *Garden party at Bethlem, 1937*
This garden party, organised by the Mental Hospital Matrons Association, was held on 24 July 1937 for delegates of the International Council of Nurses. Miss Sarah Hearder, matron of Bethlem and hon. treasurer of the Association, is seen here talking to guests.

185 (bottom right) *Garden party, 1937: the band in front of the cricket pavilion*

186 *Aerial photograph of the Monks Orchard site, taken for the 700th anniversary in 1947*
Only 17 years after the hospital was built, the skilful use of existing trees on the site gives the impression of fully matured landscaping.

The administration, static since the 1570s, has changed since 1948 from a Board of Governors, to a Special Health Authority, to the present Bethlem and Maudsley NHS Trust. Even the name, preserved for over 40 years in the rather ponderous 'Bethlem Royal Hospital and The Maudsley Hospital', has recently been subsumed under 'The Maudsley' which is now used for the whole organisation, though Bethlem as a separate entity retains its own name.

Specialist services within the joint organisation which are based at Bethlem now include a Mother and Baby Unit, Eating Disorders Unit, Drug Treatment and Rehabilitation Units, Child and Adolescent Units, and the Denis Hill (forensic psychiatry) Unit. Clinical and research teams collaborate to investigate and treat a range of disorders including psychosis, neurosis, depression, Alzheimer's disease, traumatic stress disorder, epilepsy, drug and alcohol addiction, autism, and behaviour disorders. The move towards community care has seen the opening of a range of community-based services in addition to the continuing in-patient facilities in both hospitals, and the Trust has recently taken over responsibility for Croydon Mental Health Services, currently based at Warlingham Park Hospital.

The most dramatic change, however, must be in treatment and research. The development since the 1950s of effective drugs for many conditions, together with a range of techniques based on psychotherapy, has revolutionised psychiatry in the second half of the 20th century. Now active treatment is often possible where, previously, spontaneous recovery was the only hope: while the advances in scientific knowledge, exemplified in the brain-imaging techniques made possible through the hospital's 'ultra-modern' Magnetic Resonance scanner, would have astonished even the scientifically optimistic Bethlem physicians of 1930, let alone the founder of the medieval priory with which this story began.

187 (above)   *The Maudsley Hospital in Denmark Hill, Camberwell*
The Maudsley, an LCC mental hospital founded through a donation of £30,000 by Dr. Henry Maudsley, was opened in 1923. It soon became a serious threat to Bethlem's previously unchallenged position, particularly in the fields of teaching and research. On the introduction of the National Health Service in 1948 the two hospitals were amalgamated, this being the only means by which Bethlem could remain a teaching hospital. Bethlem's new site and ancient endowments were its principal contribution to this marriage of convenience.

188 (top right)   *The Institute of Psychiatry, De Crespigny Park*
In 1948 the medical school and research arm of the Maudsley (subsequently Bethlem and Maudsley) became a constituent body of the British Postgraduate Medical Federation, as the Institute of Psychiatry. It moved into this new building next to the Maudsley in 1967.

189 (bottom right)   *Bethlem's administration unit seen from the gate, 1950s*
Apart from the lamp posts this view is relatively unchanged, though now somewhat obscured by new traffic barriers and signs.

190   *Sports day, 1955*

191   *A tutorial group outside the nurses' home, c.1956*
The lawn on which this group sits is now a staff car park. The nurses' home itself, renamed Alexandra House in 1980, was closed in 1994 and the building now houses clinical units and offices. (Female nurses began wearing uniform in 1891. It was gradually abandoned in the early 1970s.)

192 *Princess Alexandra during a visit to the archives, 1980*
Princess Alexandra succeeded her mother, Princess Marina, as patron of the joint hospital in 1969. Seen here in the conservation room of the archives department, she is being shown some bookbinding tools by the conservator, Richard Cross.

193 *The garden of Gresham House, April 1985*

194 *The Magnetic Resonance Imaging (MRI) department at the Maudsley*
Professor Nigel Leigh (right) and Steve Williams, with the MRI scanner.

195 *(overleaf)* *1997*
Some early images from a project which is currently under way at Bethlem Hospital, in which patients work under the guidance of a photographer-in-residence.

111

DYING INSIDE
TOO FULL TO
EAT

FOOLS MAT

ISHING, WANTING
TO GROW

Index

Page numbers are in plain type, illustrations in bold: references to the latter are to the text of the captions. *See also* List of Illustrations, for the subjects illustrated.

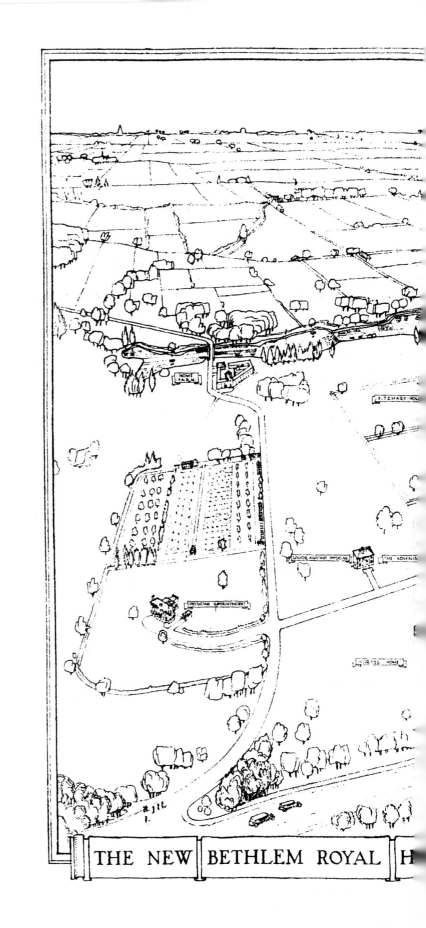

THE NEW BETHLEM ROYAL H